LEAN
ACCELERATOR

LEAN
ACCELERATOR

Lessons and Stories
from five early-stage startups

ERIC MORROW

Lean Accelerator
Copyright © 2014 by Eric Morrow. All rights reserved.
First Print Edition: December 2014
ISBN-13: 978-1505552911
ISBN-10: 1505552915

Editors: Adi Segal and Dave Terry
Cover: Julia Tamasy
Formatting: Blue Valley Author Services

No part of this book may be reproduced, scanned, or distributed in any printed or electronic form without permission. Please do not participate in or encourage piracy of copyrighted materials in violation of the author's rights. Thank you for respecting the hard work of this author.

TABLE OF CONTENTS

Always start with a good story	1
Overall structure of the Summer Accelerator	3
From drawing ideas to financial models to investor pitches	10
Accelerator Day 0—Team Blog Posts	12
Agenda for kicking off a startup accelerator	22
Class 1, Week 1—Introduction to the business model canvas	24
The precommitment mechanism for accountability in the Summer Accelerator	28
Class 2, Week 1—Legal matters and good experiments	34
Accelerator Week 1—Team Blog Posts	36
Class 3, Week 2—Value prop and invalidated hypotheses	47
Class 4, Week 2—Scrum, Agile, and Kanban	52
Accelerator Week 2—Team Blog Posts	56
Class 5, Week 3—Customer segments and Lean Startup experiments	64
Class 6, Week 3—Customer acquisition	69
Accelerator Week 3—Team Blog Posts	72
MVP examples from the real world	83
Class 7, Week 4—Customer channels	88
Class 8, Week 4—Pitching!	93
Accelerator Week 4—Team Blog Posts	95
Class 9, Week 5—Customer relationships	105
Class 10, Week 5—Digital marketing (paid ads focus)	109
Accelerator Week 5—Team Blog Posts	112
Class 11, Week 6—Revenue streams	122
Class 12, Week 6—Storyboarding	125
Accelerator Week 6—Team Blog Posts	128
Class 13, Week 7—Partners	142
Class 14, Week 7—Writing for the web	144
Accelerator Week 7—Team Blog Posts	149
Class 15, Week 8—Resources, activities, and costs	152
From Launch Pad to Demo Day	155
Lessons Learned	158
Demo Day	166
Life after the Accelerator	169
Acknowledgments	170
Appendix	171

For better or worse, there's only one way to learn from experience.

LEAN ACCELERATOR

LESSONS AND STORIES FROM FIVE EARLY-STAGE STARTUPS

by Eric Morrow
with contributions from
Caitlin J. Zuerker
Casey Scull
Cooper B. Cadle
Dillon D. Carroll
Ethan T. Van Meter
Jeffrey Terry
Logan Walker
Megan Walsh
Meghan E. Saunders
Nathan Robertson
Ali Hajimirza
Shelby W. Vanhooser
Stephen P. Soroosh

ALWAYS START WITH A GOOD STORY

A startup named Park Ave joined the University of Oklahoma Sooner Launch Pad summer accelerator ("Summer Accelerator") with a plan to build a marketplace for the buyers and sellers of private parking spaces. The idea was to have people register their private parking spots for short-term renting and then have parkers reserve and pay for spots, all through an app. It was a nice idea except that it lacked one crucial thing: **no one seemed to want to use it!** The team ran multiple experiments in the market designed to test people's willingness to either list their own parking spots or rent existing parking spots, and they couldn't find any interested users.

The best part is the unexpected

In one of the team's final experiments, they pitched their parking app product to the director of parking services at the University of Oklahoma ("OU"). When he stated that he wasn't interested, they asked one of my favorite questions: *"Is there anything you're having trouble with that you'd like help solving?"* The director said that he was having trouble measuring the usage rates of the 20 campus parking lots. At the time, he would dispatch a small army of employees to count the number of cars in spots multiple times a year. A tool that gave him better visibility of parking lot usage at an affordable price was something he would be interested in buying.

Entrepreneurs have two jobs

Entrepreneurs launching a new business should do two main things with their time—(1) ask potential customers lots of open-ended questions to better understand their needs, wants, and desires, and (2) propose solutions in exchange for cash or time commitments. After having found a potential market, the entrepreneur should propose a pilot or beta in which the customer pays the entrepreneur to start developing the potential product. By working closely with the customer, the entrepreneur builds a product or service the customer actually wants to use.

A repeatable and scalable process

In the summer of 2014, five teams of OU students went through the Summer Accelerator, a ten-week program that turned their initial ideas into practical businesses with a few early customers. The core of the Summer Accelerator curriculum was Steve Blank's Lean Launchpad, which introduced the business model canvas and validation testing. The teams, including Park Ave, followed an Agile weekly cycle. They committed to running two or three experiments a week that were designed to test their most pressing concerns and assumptions with experiential prototypes. At the beginning, the experiments tested demand for the product. Later, the experiments evolved to examine which channels the business would use to acquire customers and whether the technology could be created for the right price.

By rapidly testing critical assumptions about value proposition, customers, and channels, the teams quickly found the beginnings of product-market fit and received clear guidance from customers. This turned into cash commitments from those customers to help develop solutions to their real problems.

The tools they learned to use are scalable and repeatable. This book captures those lessons and enables anyone with a business idea to gain traction and paying customers.

OVERALL STRUCTURE OF THE SUMMER ACCELERATOR

In the summer of 2014 I worked with five startup teams from the University of Oklahoma. The Center for Entrepreneurship and the Center for the Creation of Economic Wealth (CCEW) came together to provide resources and space for the teams. I created the overall structure of the Summer Accelerator and set up or taught the classes.

Program philosophy

The basic underpinnings of the Summer Accelerator followed Steve Blank's customer development methodology called Lean Launchpad.[1] The Lean Launchpad is a ten-week program that uses the business model canvas[2] ("canvas") to guide the startup's development. Each week the teams in the Startup Accelerator watched a 30-minute video to introduce them to that week's section of the canvas.

I also emphasized the concept of prototyping in Blank's curriculum. Blank relies heavily on customer interviews for new product development. I recommended that startups show experiential prototypes to potential customers in order to get honest feedback. An experiential prototype is most easily explained by what it is not. It is not a mock-up of whatever the final product will look and feel like. Instead, it models the *experience* of what it will be like to use some

---

[1] https://www.udacity.com/course/ep245
[2] http://www.amazon.com/Business-Model-Generation-Visionaries-Challengers/dp/0470876417/

part of the final product and answers a specific product development question.

Lean Startup calls these "minimum viable products," or MVPs. In short, we want to learn as much as possible every time we talk to a customer. The problem is, your customers may not be perfectly honest even while you try to build something for them.[3] People are not malicious, it is just that they want to be supportive and tell you what you want to hear. Often, they are also bad judges of what they would actually buy if given the opportunity. For example, the Park Ave team got great feedback from potential customers and businesses when they asked if they would use their app, although in the end, no one actually ended up using it. Prototypes, or experiments, are the best way around this problem, and **this book is devoted to explaining how the five teams used experiments to find paying customers**.

OU provided each startup team with $10,000 in seed capital to fund the development of these experiential prototypes (and cover living expenses).

Each week of the Summer Accelerator we spent one class period (Tuesday morning) working on more theoretical aspects of customer development that Blank covers in his videos (related to the business model canvas); the other class period (Thursday morning) we spent working on more practical skills, such as interviewing without leading, digital marketing, storyboarding, and the Lean startup iterative development. I adapted the Thursday classes to my students' needs as we went along: there was no pre-set curriculum. Outside of class time, students worked on their product and spoke with their potential customers.

Here's the teacher's handbook I followed for the course: Lean Launchpad[4].

Every week each team wrote a one-page blog post covering the experiments the team ran, what pivots they made, which customers they spoke with, and how the team felt about their progress and

---

3 For more on this problem, check out this fun, but unreasonably expensive book, The Mom Test. http://www.amazon.com/The-Mom-Test-customers-business/dp/1492180742/
4 http://www.slideshare.net/sblank/lean-launchpad-educators-handbook-sept-2013

learning. I also wrote a post each week that I put on my blog that covered how I felt about the Summer Accelerator's progress and whether the students absorbed what I taught.

Finally, each team was matched with a mentor who had experience in the startup's industry. The mentor would spend an hour a month in person with the team, and there would be a weekly phone check-in. Ultimately, the students would meet twice a week for class for ten weeks, once a week for team dinners, and once a month with their mentors. The ten-week program culminated in Demo Day, in which the teams pitched their ideas to members of the community.

Tuesday—How the Lean Launchpad class worked

Each week the Tuesday class followed the same format.

1. Last week's experiments: Teams started by presenting their progress from the previous week, in particular, a discussion of the experiments they ran. These were presented in the same format as the blog post discussed below (**Hypothesis—Experiment—Results—Action**).

2. Business Model Canvas: Discussion began with the Steve Blank Udacity videos.[5] I kept a short list of points I wanted to make sure we covered but let the teams drive the conversation. The goal of each class was to help the students understand how their business can make money and to help them overcome any obstacles they were facing.

The nine elements of the business model canvas are as follows:[6]

1. Value proposition
2. Customer segments
3. Channels
4. Customer relationship
5. Revenue streams
6. Partners
7. Key activities
8. Key resources
9. Costs

---

5 https://www.udacity.com/course/viewer#!/c-ep245/
6 http://en.wikipedia.org/wiki/Business_Model_Canvas

OVERALL STRUCTURE OF THE SUMMER ACCELERATOR

Taken as a whole, these boxes/elements describe how a business makes money. The canvas also served as a repository for the validated and invalidated assumptions of the businesses. These assumptions were what the teams were designing experiments to test.

3. Set up new experiments: Each week the bulk of the team's efforts were spent running experiments to validate their assumptions, primarily with their potential customers. Because it is critical to have good experiments in place, I had the teams present their experiments each week so they could be refined before being executed. Both the class and I gave feedback on the setup of each experiment.

One key factor of a successful experiment is committing ahead of time to what looks like a pass (green light) or a fail (red light). If a test or experiment passes, the team should feel comfortable moving forward. More importantly, if the test fails, the team should feel comfortable closing down that assumption, hypothesis, or line of reasoning. This was essentially a verbal contract and kept the teams accountable to themselves, the program, and myself.[7]

Agile development

Agile methodology recommends breaking down big problems into smaller problems that can be worked on over a finite and normally short period of time. These are called **sprints**. I decided to run the accelerator on a weekly sprint. There were a variety of benefits to doing this—foremost for me was having the students learn the importance of not procrastinating, defining progress, locking in customer feedback, and keeping up morale.

How the rest of the week went

Each Wednesday we had a class dinner at a local restaurant with a guest from the entrepreneurship field. I tried to bring in folks from across the spectrum. We hosted recent graduates who were working at startups, local early-stage investors, and experienced entrepreneurs

---

7 For more, see **The pre-commitment mechanism for accountability in the Summer Accelerator**

who had successfully started companies. At each dinner we followed the same format. The guest was invited to give a brief introduction of who they were and what they were doing. Then each team had five minutes to give a pitch. Since we were in a restaurant, the teams couldn't use any slides or props. The guest then had five minutes to ask the team anything they wanted, and in this way, we incrementally improved each team's pitch over the ten-week program. Finally, the teams were given the chance for a general Q&A with the guest over dinner.

On Thursdays, we had "startup skills" workshops. I wasn't entirely sure what the content of these workshops would be going into the program. The only constant was that they would follow my general teaching methodology of delivering short snippets of information followed by group exercises to really engage learning. In the end, we covered the following topics during these classes (names in parentheses were guest teachers for that class):

1. Legal matters and Lean Startup experiments (Doug Branch)
2. Scrum and Agile methodologies (Dillon Carroll)
3. Customer acquisition
4. Pitching
5. Digital marketing, paid ads focus
6. Storyboarding
7. Writing for the web
8. Accounting (Pat Jones)
9. Financial modeling (Doug Woodward)

An example Pivot and Pilot

One key step I asked all the teams to take was to get a **paid pilot** in place. That meant **a customer who was interested enough in the project that they would be willing to pay money for it, even if it wasn't fully ready**. This was a critical step because a team wouldn't really know what a customer wanted until they tried to sell her something. The team learned two important things by working closely with a customer who was willing to pay to test a product or service before it was complete: first, that there was real demand for the potential product; and second, what the solution would actually look like.

A great example was Park Ave. They came into the Summer Accelerator with an idea to be a middleman parking app. People looking to sell spots in front of their home or business for a football game would post the parking spot on the app, and parkers would reserve their spot through the app. It sounded like a great idea, until they went and tested it. They couldn't find anyone who was willing to sign up to use the service—even for free! Not a promising start.

After a few more experiments, they decided to test a different idea, aka: **a pivot**. One of the team members had a technology he was working on that would let parking lot owners know the usage rates on their lots. They decided to target universities (a natural fit, since they were on a university), and sent a cold email to 20 directors of parking at universities less than a two-hour drive away from Norman, OK. Within minutes they had gotten a 50% response rate asking for more info! Now that was a warm lead on a business idea. At that moment they started going down the parking lot usage path and have found a lot more success. Their first big win was getting $10,000 from OU Parking Services to pilot their new product.

The central purpose of the Summer Accelerator was to get product-market fit. Ideas that startups have about what customers want are rarely, if ever, correct straight out of the gate. It is only by working directly with customers and using experiential prototypes to get honest feedback that startups can understand how to make things that people actually want to buy or use.

Preparing for day 1

In addition to the first round of videos, I also gave the students one article to read for the first day of class: "Looking for Customers? Be a Hunter, Not a Gatherer."[8] The article describes the mindset I asked the students to adopt, one that is critical for early-stage startups,

---

8 http://www.fastcolabs.com/3015583/open-company/looking-for-customers-be-a-hunter-not-a-gatherer

or anyone launching a new product or service. Most people get so carried away with their good idea they forget to ask if anyone actually wants it. Hunting down potential customers early will provide good feedback on whether the product being developed will ever actually be purchased and used. And it provides the great secondary goal of being the source of information to change (pivot) the product, which inevitably happens as a team works more closely with their customers.

That's it! It's go time.

FROM DRAWING IDEAS TO FINANCIAL MODELS TO INVESTOR PITCHES

Normally my problem with early-stage startups is that all of their developers' dreams and visions are unsupported by any data. When they make pitches, they are asking me to suspend my disbelief and engage with them in flights of fancy. My interest is in proving a startup's ability to deliver value to a customer and make money. Over the course of my summer of running this startup accelerator at the University of Oklahoma, I've fleshed out what I think is an effective process for accumulating the data to make a successful pitch to investors or an internal team about how a business will operate.

Draw your business model

It all starts with drawing—drawing a business model. The advantage of drawing is that everyone understands how to draw without need of further explanation. Therefore it is a tool accessible to anyone. And it has the further advantage of simplifying things for experienced entrepreneurs. As Steve Blank repeats often in his Lean Launchpad curriculum, if you can't draw it, you don't understand it.

Transfer to the business model canvas

After drawing comes the business model canvas. The canvas is split into nine boxes that, when taken together, explain how a business makes money. More interesting from a startup's perspective is that each of the boxes contains specific information, much of which pertains to assumptions made at the outset. So the canvas is a useful tool for cataloging a startup's assumptions and helping the team keep track of which assumptions need to be tested.

Testing assumption day by day

Going from an overall picture of what the startup looks like to the day-to-day activities, the startup can make use of being lean, agile, and using a Kanban board. Lean describes how to run experiments using the build-measure-learn cycle and experiential prototypes/MVPs. Agile speaks to a weekly cycle and breaking down the massive amount of work that goes into launching a company into more manageable and smaller chunks. And Kanban is the tool that keeps the startup team on track and making progress against a specific set of activities.

Create a financial model

Once the critical assumptions are tested, I think the final piece of the puzzle is the financial model, as expressed in an Excel spreadsheet. The advantage of the spreadsheet is that it allows the team to change the variables and get a look at what the impact on the top and bottom lines would be.

The part I like best about the financial model is that changes to aspects of the model are just assumptions about how the business will work. Startup teams following this methodology already have the tools (from lean) about how to test assumptions, so any change in the financial model can quickly be tested for validity.

ACCELERATOR DAY 0—TEAM BLOG POSTS

A brief introduction to the teams

All members of the various teams were current students at the University of Oklahoma or were recent graduates. They came from a broad background of academic disciplines, including mechanical and software engineering, marketing, public relations, business, and entrepreneurship. Teams ranged in size from one to five. Some teams had begun work on their project during the school year and so had about six months of experience working together. Others started the first day of the program!

- **Levaté** focused on building a mechanical device that can vertically lift wheelchair users.

- **Driven Analytics** worked on collecting usage data from cars and selling it to dealerships to assist with marketing efforts.

- **Sowers Publishing** looked into making a better and more customizable Bible.

- **Icarus Aerial Technologies** explored using drone photography in a variety of industries.

- **Park Ave** (later **Project Xip**) tackled making parking easier and more efficient.

Team blog posts

I have included in this book the weekly blog posts the teams wrote as they went through the Summer Accelerator.

The blogs (mostly) followed this format:

Hypothesis: Here's what we thought.
Experiment: Here's what we did to test that thought.
Results: Here's what we found out.
Action: Here's what we want to do next.

The purpose of including the blogs is to give readers insight into the hearts and minds of the startup teams as they went through the challenges of launching a company that customers care about. For the most part, the blogs are unedited, although I have redacted certain personal details. I also have left in the pictures the students included. Due to black and white printing constraints, as well as the photos originating from iPhones, the quality makes them hard to read. I decided to include the photos anyway, simply to illustrate the type of work the students were doing.

The following posts are what the teams wrote coming into the first class.

Levaté

The State of the LLC: Levaté

The inaugural CCEW Agile Product Design team, which ideated, prototyped, and validated Levaté as a product and a business, left the SLP Accelerator team in a good position to make rapid progress over the 10 weeks of the program. After ideating the product, the work the team did can be broadly divided into three categories: *customer discovery*, *prototyping*, and *commercialization*.

Customer Discovery

Over the course of the semester, team Levaté conducted over 10 in-depth interviews with wheelchair users (potential customers) and over

20 interviews with industry experts. Additionally, the team collected over 40 survey responses to judge customer feedback about the price and initial feature set of Levaté. At a $1000 price point, 18 of the 40 said they would definitely (4), probably (4), or maybe (10) buy Levaté.

The team also made use of experiential prototyping with around 5 wheelchair users to identify key design objectives and constraints. For example, by incrementally attaching weights to the bottom of the users' wheelchairs, the team determined the weight constraint of 10 lbs. Additional tests identified the need to lift the entire chair as opposed to just the seat, a "sweet spot" lift of 12 inches (enough to reach most cabinets and counters but not too much to be unsafe or make the users uncomfortable), and the need for an easily attachable device with a preference towards a quick-release clasp mechanism.

Moving forward, the team will be focusing on having more conversations with wheelchair dealers to build preliminary relationships. We will also be using the prototypes (described below) to elicit more meaningful feedback from potential customers, with the end goal of selling later-stage prototypes to customers.

Prototyping

The team applied Agile techniques to make 4 functional prototypes over the course of 8 weeks. Of those 4, two captured elements of the design the team is moving forward with. One illustrated the use of PVC pipes of varying diameter to create a telescoping pneumatic cylinder. Unfortunately, the inability to adequately seal the PVC pipe hamstrung the prototype. Another prototype, using a prebuilt, non-telescoping pneumatic cylinder, effectively demonstrated the concept of a pneumatic lift device attached via quick-clasps, although it lacked the full 12 inches of lift ability.

Moving forward, the team will be iteratively building prototypes to perform the following functions:

- Lift the chair 12 inches off the ground stably and quickly; ie, doesn't wobble

- Maintains the lift position until user disengages device
- Harnesses spinning of wheels to fill compressed air chamber underneath chair
- Stores enough compressed air to lift the chair X number of times consecutively
- Attaches and detaches within 5 seconds

Commercialization

The team has identified a market of 125,000 active wheelchair users as the ideal customer, as they are more likely than most to be in unadapted environments on a regular basis. To reach these customers, Levaté will sell its devices to custom wheelchair dealers, who typically recommend and sell accessories to users in addition to fitting them with new chairs every 4-6 years. An urban area of >1,000,000 people typically has 30-40 wheelchair dealers alone. At a selling price of $1,000, dealers will take a 25% commission, or $250 of each device sold.

The team developed a preliminary financial model that projects up to $9.5M in profit over 5 years and 19,000 lives impacted, assuming a 15% target market (125,000 total active users) over those 5 years. This 15% penetration figure has been validated by the results of user's surveys, conversations with 10 dealers and an accessory manufacturer. Levaté will reach this saturation point by employing a sales force that will expand to 8 salespeople by its 5th year of operation. These salespeople will directly target wheelchair dealers. Additional marketing will be done at industry conferences and trade shows and through advertisements online and in industry journals and catalogs.

Moving forward, the team will focus on the concrete steps needed to commercialize Levaté as a product. This includes taking steps to apply for a patent, particularly on the "wheel-powered design"; taking necessary steps to organize a small scale user study (needed to convince wheelchair dealers to carry Levaté as a product in their stores); and eventually, complete the fabrication specifications for the final design and contract with a manufacturer to begin a production run of Levaté.

Driven Analytics

Driven Analytics is very excited to be starting the Sooner Launch Pad accelerator program this week! We have made a lot of progress in April and May, including winning nearly $30,000 in seed funds in three different business plan pitch competitions.

Oklahoma Gov Cup: $12,000

We placed second in the high growth graduate track of the Oklahoma Gov Cup in mid April, as well as taking first place in the interview portion of the competition. Our second place finish made us eligible to compete at the Tri-State competition in May in Las Vegas.

OU New Venture Pitch Competition: $1,250

Also in mid April, Jake and I traveled up to Tulsa to compete in the New Venture Pitch competition, sponsored by the Sooner Launch Pad. We placed second, winning $1,250, which, although disappointing, was a great learning experience. We encountered a number of very difficult judging situations and used that opportunity to learn how to better convey our value propositions and how to help judges that may not have deep technological or automotive knowledge understand what we are doing.

California Dreaming: $16,000

In late April, Rachel, Mitchell and I traveled to Orange County, California, to participate in the California Dreaming pitch competition, sponsored by Chapman University. This competition was an amazing experience because all of the judges were actual investors from VC groups and teams were being judged on the viability of their company, rather than the more academic exercise of producing a business plan. Although we didn't advance to the semifinals in the long form pitch competition after the first day, we did match with our favorite VC firm during the speed dating event. In the speed dating event, six VC firms spent five minutes with each of six teams, and at the end, each team and each judge secretly chose who they would be most interested in spending more time with. We chose the Pritzker Group, a $400M fund in the LA area, and they also chose us. By "matching," we won a free consulting session with the Pritzker Group! We will be having our consulting session at the end of May.

Although we didn't advance after the first day, we were still eligible to compete for $6,000 in the case competition, as well as $10,000 in the 90 second fast pitch competition on the second day. We stayed up late that night and put together our case, taking a risky but innovative approach to the case that was provided. The next day, our risk paid off as we advanced to the finals for the case competition and went on to take first place. In the 90 second fast pitch competition, I gave the pitch, and we not only advanced but also took first place! Overall, we were very excited with our performance and it was a great learning experience.

As we start in the SLP accelerator this week, we have a lot of stuff on our plate. Jake, Mitchell and I leave on Thursday morning for Vegas to compete for $30,000 at the Tri-State competition, and this is our main focus this week. After we return from Tri-State, week two will be focused on successfully pulling down data from the three SmartDrive Alpha devices that we currently have on vehicles and successfully processing that data into meaningful information. In week three and four, our focus will turn to working directly with one of the four dealerships that expressed an interested to be involved in a pilot test with us. We realized that we need to do a LOT of work to actually hone in on the way we present data and information to both car owners and to car dealerships, and we feel like the best way to do this will be to get a control group of 10 new car buyers that are willing to meet with us throughout the summer and help us find that product-market fit. By working with a dealership, we can hone the product-market fit on both sides of the market at the same time, with the goal of actually getting the 10 car owners to pay us money by the end of the summer to continue their service with Driven Analytics and SmartDrive.

In addition to working on our product market fit, we have a lot of administrative work that needs to be done, including hashing out operating agreements, making any needed adjustments to our corporate filing statues, getting our bank account open and beginning to heavily focus on protecting our intellectual property. It will be a busy summer: we are really excited and are hitting the ground running!

In conclusion, I just want to harken back to one of the first inspirational moments we had as a team as we were gearing up for submitting our business plan to the Rice Business Plan competition. After some long nights working on the plan, we were almost done, and in a text to us all Rachel coined the phrase "Go-Drive-Win." I think that phrase is very fitting once again as we start the adventure of launching Driven Analytics…it is time to Go…Drive and WIN!

Sowers Publishing

Cooper happened upon this idea about four months ago and since then we have spent most of our time simply researching the problem, the possible solutions, and our target market. This past semester we were in our first segment of the new venture development process where we were challenged to dream in every possible direction and create solutions, not exactly taking into account how feasible those dreams might be. Outside of class, our professor challenged us to quantify a market for this product, proving to potential investors that there truly is a need for a customizable Bible. We have spent hours researching and talking to people, but we have been limited in being able to create actual prototypes because of the limitations of the copyrighted versions of the Bible. During our research we were able to survey around 30 people, and over 90% of them said the most important feature in a Bible they looked at was the version. Without the ability to offer customers the version they want, our market is immediately limited to the specific versions we can offer and how many people purchase that version. Cooper had the chance to sit down with a friend that works for Mardel, which is one of the largest Christian bookstores in the world. Not only are they excited about this idea, they want to discuss the potential opportunity for a strategic partnership. Having them on our side would give us access to all copyright privileges as well as assisting our immediate branding. In addition, this would help position us so as to limit potential competitors. This is extremely important, as none of our ideas to date are considered intellectual property. We have drawn up the documents to file for incorporating Sowers Publishing Group as a Limited Liability Company.

Going into the first week, our company is preparing to file our incorporation paperwork at the state capital. This will also be our first week putting together our initial business model canvas. Our next order of business will be setting up a second meeting with our connection at Mardel to figure out what steps we need to take to gain access to the different versions of the Bible. Looking forward to prototyping, we will also be scheduling meetings with printers and binders to figure out the different costs of each aspect of the process. We would love to lock down a printer and binder by the end of next week so that we can start building minimal viable products. Next, we are going to create (or combine) our rolodex to begin a detailed customer list. Finally, we hope to have our operating agreement in place by the end of this week.

By the end of this summer, we hope to be comfortable enough with our business model canvas to begin software development for our website. We want to secure a partnership with both a printer and binder so that we can begin selling and production. Ideally, by the end of the program we would like to begin developing a marketing strategy focused on OU students, specifically, those involved in popular ministries. Many of these students have already expressed interest, along with the dozens of staff members associated with these ministries. In a perfect world, we will begin marketing to the general public starting in January of 2015.

Icarus Aerial Technologies

Icarus Aerial Technologies was birthed in Logan Walker's Media Entrepreneurship class as a semester-long business development project. Casey Scull joined Icarus toward the end of the semester. We have a shared interest in the commercial drone industry and want to be an industry leader as the commercial uses emerge. We think our strengths in marketing, branding, risk assessment and financial planning as well as our passion for technology will help position us for success.

We are on the precipice of a rush to commercial drone use in the United States. The potential uses for drones are many, but we have chosen to focus on agriculture as our primary consumer. The potential uses in the agricultural industry are legion, and we see a viable long-term business opportunity there. We also have some opportunities in the real estate market via local connections in this industry. The real estate market would be an easy area to enter the marketplace and caters to Logan's strength as a videographer, photographer, voice-over talent and editor. Other companies have found success here as well.

Ultimately, success for Icarus Aerial Technologies is finding the right consumer and offering that consumer the right services. Currently, commercial drone use is a wide-open and undeveloped market. We could go many directions with our company at this stage. Our challenge will be to find the place where drone technology serves as the best long-term solution to a major consumer pain. Once we find our consumer, we can tailor our drones and their peripheral technologies to be the ultimate solution to the consumers' issues. We can also expand our services into other industries once we have started to become profitable and well known in our first market. We expect to be iterating constantly this summer as we find our consumer and outfit our product.

Park Ave

Park Ave is our web and mobile application connecting buyers and sellers of event parking. Park Ave over the past semester has gone through an iterative process of narrowing our target market and isolating core features our customers have been shown to need. Currently, we have a workable prototype web and iOS application that is approaching the Beta testing stage, and while this software has been shown to work amongst the developers, it is far from perfect. Testing the software for robustness will also be key to ensure an elegant experience for the users.

Additionally, we see a need to create a marketing strategy to acquire customers in our "donut" region around events where visibility for sellers of parking is low enough to justify the use of our service and where buyers would still be willing to purchase parking and walk to the event. We have a general idea of how to go about this, but further research and validation would be immensely beneficial. Moving forward, Park Ave will need to incorporate/file for recognition and enter into all appropriate agreements with the University before generating revenue, and this will be a key step to execute before we start charging customers. Testing software is one thing, but registering a server under a corporate name and charging people's credit cards is quite another.

AGENDA FOR KICKING OFF A STARTUP ACCELERATOR

For the official launch of the Summer Accelerator, I invited all the team members and all of the faculty and administration responsible for putting together the program to an assembly, followed by lunch. I had an idea of what we needed to accomplish (introduce ourselves, answer student questions, map out the summer), but I didn't have a proper agenda. In the true spirit of learning and entrepreneurship, I discovered that was a mistake! So here's the agenda I wish I had made before the kickoff.

Agenda for Accelerator kickoff

1. Intro from Jim Wheeler, director of the Center for Entrepreneurship—why we are all here
2. Intro from the CCEW team—lots of staff supporting the Accelerator, what they all do
3. Intro from guests—I wasn't sure if there were going to be any guests/mentors, but we ended up having some, so they told us who they were, too
4. Intros from teams—short statement of each team's business idea, plus individual introductions from each of the team members
5. Goal setting question for teams—where are you now and what would success look like ten weeks from now

AGENDA FOR KICKING OFF A STARTUP ACCELERATOR

6. Explain calendar for summer—what a weekly cadence will look like, what the end goal of the Accelerator is (Demo Day)
7. Discuss legal matters—organization of business plus promissory note
8. Introduce role of mentors—each team has a mentor, get to meet three times
9. Site logistics—parking, door access
10. Take any questions—dress code came up
11. Go have lunch!

CLASS 1, WEEK 1—INTRODUCTION TO THE BUSINESS MODEL CANVAS

Here is the first thing I said to my group of five teams when I started the first of 20 workshops for the summer:

> *You are CEOs. I'm a guide. You are not working for me. You are working for yourself. If you don't feel like something is helping your business succeed, tell me. This Accelerator is for you, and I want to make it as useful and effective as it can be.*

Getting into startup mode

The goal of the first class is to get the teams into "startup" mode. That means out of "school" mode, where they are supposed to be giving the right answer. That means out of "planning" mode, where they work on writing business plans and whiteboarding ideas. It means focusing exclusively on testing their product ideas with real customers. In short, customer development.

Setting the table

I started with a discussion of the Steve Blank Udacity videos on what it means to launch a startup. I asked the very general question—"What did you get from the videos?"

The key topics I wanted to cover were as follows:

- **Search vs execution**—startups are looking (searching) for a business model, while established businesses are executing on a proven business model.

- **Model vs plan**—A business model describes, with the business model canvas, how a business will run and make money. A plan describes why you're in business.

- **Business model canvas**—"The Business Model Canvas is a strategic management and Lean Startup template for developing new or documenting existing business models. It is a visual chart with elements describing a firm's value proposition, infrastructure, customers, and finances."[9]

And the following terminology:

- **Hypothesis**—a statement about what you believe to be true that can be proven false.

- **Experiment**—any activity that will allow you to prove or disprove the hypothesis.

- **Customer development**—interacting with potential customers to build a product they care about and want to use or pay for.

Drawing your business model

After a brief discussion, we launched into our first exercise, "Drawing Your Business Model." A key challenge in drafting a business model, which Jim Wheeler and I had discussed, is that the business model canvas is not intuitive. We suggested having teams draw out their business model, thinking about what they needed to buy to make their product and to whom they would sell it. After each team drew their business model, I went over how to translate the drawing to the business model canvas. The key was to follow the money!

---

9 http://en.wikipedia.org/wiki/Business_Model_Canvas

CLASS 1, WEEK 1—INTRODUCTION TO THE BUSINESS MODEL CANVAS

The primary purpose of the business model canvas at this point was to list out the startup's assumptions. Common ones for early stage startups are (1) people want to buy/use what we are selling, and (2) we can actually make/produce the product. Once teams can identify which assumptions are most critical for their business, they know what to tackle. I emphasized testing/validating the critical stuff, not the easy-to-test stuff. That meant all of the startups in the room were going to address the two issues listed above first.

Presenting the business model

After the drawing exercise, each group presented their business model, in words, to the class. And the students offered feedback. The goal of this exercise was to get teams in the habit of practicing their pitching/explaining of their business—can't do that enough! Another goal was to get the other people in the room thinking critically about business models. It is often much simpler to look at someone else's work with a critical eye, and through the critique build up the analytical muscles that will serve them well throughout the startup process.

Testing assumptions!

Then we started getting into my favorite topic: how will we test? Who do we need to talk to? The teams mapped out their strategy for week 1, with the understanding that Class 2 of Week 1 would focus on Lean Startup methodology and developing the experiment they would run later in the week.

I had the teams choose a tool to share their results with me—ie: Dropbox, Evernote, or Google Drive. Steve Blank offers his Lean Launchpad software to have startups track their process through the curriculum. One student in the class said that he had used the Lean Launchpad software for a class but chose not to continue with it after the class had ended. I decided to let the teams use whichever tool they were most comfortable with to track their progress and that they would continue using after the Accelerator ended.

CLASS 1, WEEK 1—INTRODUCTION TO THE BUSINESS MODEL CANVAS

I followed the Y Combinator (a leading accelerator responsible for Airbnb and Dropbox) model of signing up for office hours to talk with me. This was to track the demand for office hours.

THE PRECOMMITMENT MECHANISM FOR ACCOUNTABILITY IN THE SUMMER ACCELERATOR

Verbal contracts

Precommitment means deciding ahead of time what you'll do if the results of a lean experiment turn out one way or the other. It was one of the most effective tools I used this summer to move five startup teams from ideas to revenue in ten weeks. In the section below, I'm going to dig deeper into the actual mechanism involved.

The start—figuring out what you want to learn

Using the Lean Startup methodology to design and run experiments is a powerful way to determine if your startup's assumptions are true or false. The standard cycle Lean Startup describes is **Build-Measure-Learn**. It means **build** an experiment, **measure** the results, and **learn** from them. This Build-Measure-Learn cycle was the core of the work the five startup teams did to validate their ideas and show they had a product or service customers would pay for. Note that I call the cycle "Hypothesis-Test-Results" in this book, which is what Blank uses for Lean Launchpad. Here's how it worked for one of the teams in the Summer Accelerator.

    Icarus Aerial Technologies spent the summer investigating potential uses for drone photography. One key issue they needed to figure out early on was which customer segment to focus on. They had heard from a variety of friends and acquaintances that certain industries, like farming and real estate, would love the opportunity to use their tech. That is an assumption that needed to be tested!

The first thing Icarus wanted to learn was whether farmers would be interested in the drone's capabilities. It's critical that the learning step (the hypothesis) is framed as a yes or no question, so it can be validated (farmers are interested) or invalidated (farmers are not interested).

The experiment—how you're going to test your assumption

Icarus then needed to figure out how to test the hypothesis. There are a few simple ways to test if someone is interested in your product, and my favorite is the Presell, or "Sell and Scramble." Lean Startup is heavily focused on not building products or services that people aren't interested in. So a good experiment will test the demand before building anything.

In this case, the experiment was for Icarus to approach ten to 20 farmers, primarily at farmers' markets, and try to get just one of them to invite the team out for a test flight. No money needed to be exchanged. Instead, Icarus was looking for a verbal commitment that they could fly over the farmer's fields. If Icarus could find one farmer, they would consider the test passed, or validated. If not, invalidated. This is a predetermined indicator of success.

The precommitment

Icarus then needed to *precommit* to what validating or invalidating the test meant. In other words, regardless of the outcome of the test, they needed to commit to what they would do next. This is very important, because frequently, a team will set up a test, invalidate the test, and then continue anyway because they felt the test didn't really do what they wanted. This is a waste of time, especially in an accelerated summer program. If the results of the test won't change the startup's mind about an assumption they hold, or if it won't change the next thing they want to do, there is no point in running the test.

I want to highlight that running tests is not about throwing ideas against the wall and seeing what sticks. Tests are designed to learn certain things (such as whether a certain customer segment is interested in a product) and to validate assumptions and hypotheses.

For Icarus, if they couldn't find one farmer out of 20 to invite them out to do a test run, it would mean that farmers were not a viable customer segment at this particular moment in time. Icarus decided that if they invalidated the experiment, they would move on to a different customer segment, probably real estate. If they validated the experiment, they would dig deeper into the needs of the farmers who had invited them to fly.

Running the experiment

This part is the most conceptually easy (just do it!) but also the most difficult. This is because everything up till now took place in the safe confines of the classroom, on the whiteboard, in discussions, and in our imagination. But experiments always happen in the real world, where I can guarantee things won't go as easily or smoothly as planned.

For Icarus, they faced the gamut of responses from the farmers they talked to. Some ignored them, others yelled at them, and still others chatted but immediately shot down their ideas. All in all, it was quite clear that the people Icarus spent the week talking to were not interested in the idea.

Another key point happened here. Icarus did not go ask people what they thought about the idea in the abstract. They tried to actually sell the service to people. They asked for firm commitments in cash and time. And they were pretty firmly shot down.

Which is actually great!

It became clear to Icarus pretty fast that the local farmers they were speaking with were not interested in their service. After spending many months doing business planning in a classroom and coming up with a "sure-fire" idea, one that was already working in other parts of the world, they got an immediate NO as soon as they approached some customers. That's why I like actually trying to sell your idea to real people as soon as possible with this experimental approach. It means you don't need to waste any more time once an assumption gets invalidated! This is good news, because it means you can spend your valuable time and resources chasing down another lead.

Precommitment is a valuable tool for focusing a startup's attentions on critical tasks and ensuring they don't waste time running tests that they won't learn from.

Adding additional insights

Validating or invalidating an assumption or hypothesis is the main point of running an experiment. But it isn't the only one. I also asked all the startup teams to share their insights from the experiment. Insights are hard to capture broadly, but they often arise from *conversations* the teams had with their potential customers *after* they were rejected. Many startups find their real business after pitching one idea and then asking one of my favorite questions after getting turned down: "What frustrations do you have that you wish I could build a solution for?"

Presenting experiments in class

Each week the startup teams came up with new experiments to run, just like the one Icarus ran with the farmers. In class the teams would present their experiments for the week on Tuesday morning. They would state very clearly:

- The hypothesis as a yes/no question
- The test they would run to validate/invalidate the hypothesis
- What success or failure looks like
- What they would do next in the case of failure, indicating what failure (invalidation) really meant

The following Tuesday we would start class with presentations of the results of the prior week's experiments. The teams would present:

- **Hypothesis**: Here's what we thought
- **Experiment**: Here's what we did to test that thought
- **Results**: Here's what we found out *(the real data!)*
- **Insights**: Here's what else we learned

Accountability and Agile

The purpose of setting up these public experiments in class is to keep everyone accountable to each other. It is hard to slack off when you know you will be accountable for what you publicly said you would do (see the book *Influence: Science and Practice*[10] for a lot more on that). What ended up happening, though, is that the teams found themselves feeling accountable to me personally rather than to the group as a whole. This works well as long as they are in the Summer Accelerator! But I wanted them to feel more accountable to each other

---

10 http://www.amazon.com/Influence-Science-Practice-ePub-5th-ebook/dp/B001CDZYVE/

during the summer as well as after, when the structure of the Summer Accelerator was removed.

What I would like to do next time is have the teams provide more critique of each others' experiments during the summer itself. I just read the Five Dysfunctions of a Team,[11] and accountability to the team as a whole is one key element. The teams are continuing to meet on a biweekly basis after the Accelerator to hold each other accountable. For example: https://www.youtube.com/watch?v=St2BhIbOLUs.

One last point to keep in mind is that I used a weekly Agile/Scrum sprint[12] to structure the Summer Accelerator. The purpose of a sprint is to predefine work that needs to be done and allow teams to manage themselves. It also sets clear goals as to *when* the works needs to be finished by. That structure allowed teams to stay on weekly sprints, biting off small pieces of work (in the form of experiments) as they went along, rather than worrying about a bigger picture that is outside their control. It also allowed the teams to make steady progress each week, which is critical for startups in time-crunch situations.

---

11 http://www.amazon.com/The-Five-Dysfunctions-Team-Leadership/dp/0787960756/
12 http://scrumethodology.com/scrum-sprint/

CLASS 2, WEEK 1—LEGAL MATTERS AND GOOD EXPERIMENTS

Good experiments

Designing good experiments is the most critical skill the student-entrepreneur needs to improve. The problems they have to avoid are (1) throwing everything at the wall to see what sticks, and (2) not completing experiments before starting new ones. It boils down to what the purpose of a startup is, and I adopted the Steve Blank definition that **a startup is searching for a business model**. The best way to search for a business model is through a series of experiments, tests, or prototypes.

Searching means discovering information, and experimentation is the best way to do that. The purpose of an experiment is to collect information—to see if a given hypothesis is right or wrong. That's why each hypothesis is framed as a yes/no question, so it can be validated/invalidated.

My goal for the summer was to have each startup team run at least one experiment per week over the life of the Accelerator. Ideally, I wanted that pace to pick up as we moved along, so that by the middle of the summer teams would have been running multiple experiments each week. We were accelerating after all! vroom vroom.

CLASS 2, WEEK 1—LEGAL MATTERS AND GOOD EXPERIMENTS

Taking care of legal matters

The second class included an introduction to the legal concerns pertaining to new startups by Doug Branch, a director and senior attorney at Phillips Murrah, in Oklahoma City. This class came very early in the Accelerator so that all the teams' companies could be properly formed and filed with the state and could receive investment from OU. Doug covered three main areas: (1) corporate formation, (2) allocation of equity, and (3) protection of intellectual property (IP). Here are the slides Doug used in class: OU SLPA Legal Workshop discussion deck.[13]

We discussed the benefits of LLC vs C Corp (go C corp if you're expecting professional investment in your company). Nearly all of my teams went the LLC route, which is easier to file for and easier to manage. We talked about equity, and at this very early stage in the game, decided to just skip setting the value of each business by using a convertible note[14] to provide the seed round. This allowed us to revisit that number when the startup was ready for a funding event. And finally, we looked at protecting IP and the importance of having employee agreements with everyone who works for the company in order for the founders to retain control of their technology.

The teams needed to have their organizations formed by week 2 of the Summer Accelerator so they could receive their university funding. One team also suggested having a checklist they could use to make sure they were doing everything properly. This is something I'd like to develop before the next Summer Accelerator in 2015.

---

13 http://ericmorrow.com/wp-content/uploads/OU-Workshop-discussion-deck.pptx
14 http://techcrunch.com/2012/04/07/convertible-note-seed-financings/

ACCELERATOR WEEK 1—TEAM BLOG POSTS

Levaté

The State of the LLC: Levaté

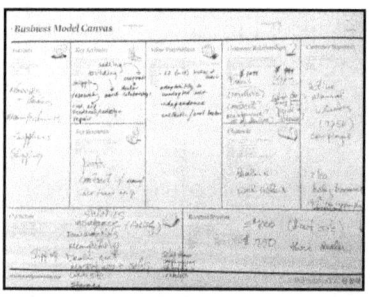

The first in the ten-part series, "Levaté Business Model Canvas." Almost as eagerly awaited as the fourth Game of Thrones *season.*

Experimentation

Hypothesis: 15% of active wheelchair users will pay a down-payment (ie, at least some money) towards a $1000 Levaté unit.
Prototype:
1. Ask 5-10 active wheelchair users: Would you buy Levaté?
2. If yes: Would you write us a check or donate on kickstarter?
3. If yes: success!

4. If no: Would you donate a bit of money—any amount you desire—as a sort of down-payment?
   5. If yes: still success!
   6. If no: Why not?

Evaluation: If 1 or more of the wheelchair users donates money to Levaté, the test is a success. If no one donates money to Levaté, the hypothesis and test will be revised according to the prevailing feedback gained from the question, Why not?

Definitive Findings From Experimenting

Inconclusive. Despite over 20 cold calls and just as many emails, only 3 customer interviews were possible. None of those 3 made advance payments, proffering lack of money as the chief reason. While believable given that all three lacked formal employment, this was still disappointing both in terms of number of responses and their hesitance to donate money.

However, these users provided further validation of the value proposition and showed their interest in the product by agreeing to do further tests and connecting Levaté with other wheelchair users and experts in the industry.

The tests agreed upon included measuring projected uses of Levaté each day for a week as well as how long wheelchair users would be willing to wheel around with 10 lbs under their chair.

Driven Analytics

Last week was a busy week between getting things going at the SLP Accelerator, further peeling back the layers of what will be involved with IP filing, discussions on forming the company and continuing to work on analyzing our data and getting our initial algorithm validated by dealerships mechanics. In addition to all of that, our team made final preparations for the Tri-State business plan competition in Las

Vegas that we attended at the end of the week. Here is what we accomplished:

- IP: After discussing our IP situation with our patent attorney for about 2 hours, we figured out what information will be needed to complete our initial filings, and those documents were completed and will be submitted this evening. Filing will be done before Friday the 30th.

- As the company has tangible cash assets to its name right now, forming has been more complicated than expected. Counsel has been made with Doug Branch (lawyer) as well as Stephen Pearce (CPA) on how we should form. The founders will be meeting this week on Wednesday night to finalize equity positions and contributions and make the final decisions on how we will form.

- Algorithm development and validation ran into two technical hurdles that are being addressed this week.

  ◊ Our server was set up running Windows 8 IIS 8.5 but this version proved to be too unstable to reliably work right now so the server was rebuilt running Windows 2008 R2 IIS 7.5. The server was rebuilt over the weekend and is currently being tested and configured.

  ◊ One of the critical metrics we need for maintenance predictions is the odometer reading, however, this PID has been locked down by OEMs in order to prevent odometer fraud. We have developed a work around, as there is a PID to count "miles since indicator reset." This, along with an initial mileage input from the customer, should allow us to count the miles, at least for now. There may be a better way to get miles, and our technical team is researching that possibility.

  ◊ Final preparations for Tri-State were made on Tuesday and Wednesday night, with the team gathering to make final changes to the presentation and to practice the pitch a number of time, honing it before leaving for Vegas. We departed on Thursday at noon and upon arrival in Vegas, spent a few final hours prepping before heading down to the reception that kicked off the event. Our presentation was Friday morning, which went very well. We felt like we got through the presentation in a very clear and professional manor, and the judges had insightful but not difficult questions. Overall, we were very happy with the performance. We went to get lunch and that evening, at the awards banquet, we were awarded 2nd place of $20,000! Although we are very happy with the victory, it does add further complication to our formation, as to date the founders have won $49,250.

This week we will continue to sort out issues with the server and the algorithms that are running on test vehicles. We hope to be able to start validating those algorithms with mechanics if at all possible. In addition, we have a meeting on Friday afternoon with the Pritzker Group, a venture capital group located in Los Angeles. The goal of this meeting is to get their input on what we are doing right and wrong and what steps we should be taking in order to make the venture more investable by the time we exit the Accelerator.

I will be in North Carolina next week but will meet with an iPhone app development company and will continue to work on our algorithms, as well as any lingering issues with regard to wrapping up formation and IP.

Business Model Drawing

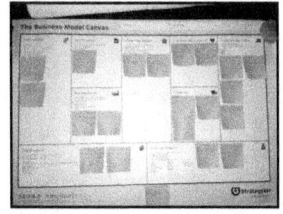

ACCELERATOR WEEK 1—TEAM BLOG POSTS

Sowers Publishing

Week 1 was an interesting blur of hitting the ground running while also trying to get our feet underneath us at the exact same time. As is the case with any startup, no matter how much you feel like you accomplish there is always so much more that needs to be done. One of the biggest take-aways from everything we learned this week was that startups are not just smaller versions of large companies, meaning that we can't do the same things they are doing and expect the same results. Our approach has to be different, and encouragement from friends and family cannot count as validating our ideas.

Another huge take-away from this week is that there is a large difference between being busy and being productive. Unless the tasks we are trying to complete help validate or invalidate our ideas, they aren't giving us a direction to move in. Before learning this, we had scheduled meetings with many different people to give us insight on the direction of the company and the logistics to get us there.

We really hit a block in the road when our prototype couldn't be printed and we had to begin building them on our own. A few hours into putting together our first Bible, we began to question the outcome of our future product. Though after we finished, the MVP looked good and seemed to feel like it will withstand wear and tear this summer. Moreover, we discovered the knowledge behind the complete process is more valuable than the money we could have spent having others build it for us. This was our first real "no" we have come across and now understand the value of learning to pivot and grow from similar situations. Ultimately, the week was more stressful than intended and required twice the time as planned, but the progress we made and validation we now hope to strive for is something we see as tangible and plan to work to accomplish.

Mentor meeting with Mr. Pat Jones (Wednesday)

We were fairly unsure of what to expect from our relationship with Mr. Jones throughout the course of this summer so we did not show up to the meeting as prepared as we should have been. It is a helpless feeling finding out that you haven't done all your "homework" right before a meeting begins, but it was a good lesson for both of us to learn because we won't make that mistake again. Whether by chance or fate, Mr. Jones is quite literally the most perfect mentor that anyone could have picked for us. With his experience as the CFO at Hobby Lobby he understands the inner workings of the organization better than anyone else could, and with his current work at Petra he has an understanding of supply chain that is crucial to our business. The best piece of advice came when Mr. Jones emphasized how important it is for entrepreneurs to understand balance sheets because it can make or break a company. No matter how many times a professor explains that, it doesn't sink in quite as much as when a successful businessman is sitting across the table emphasizing it as well. The advice and feedback from this meeting was helpful moving forward because Mr. Jones offered advice and several suggestions that we had not thought of.

Logo meeting with Matt Stansberry (Thursday)

One of the things that Cooper and I have wanted to do from the beginning is "brand" our company. In retrospect, this is not incredibly important for where we are currently, but it will be down the road. We contacted several local designers a few weeks ago and just asked for a few minutes of their time to discuss their services and pricing. On Wednesday following our meeting with Mr. Jones, we went to lunch with Matt Stansberry, a local designer. Matt was able to tell us about his work and how his company operated, which was fun for both Cooper and myself because we enjoy the relational side of business. The more we learn the more we reflect, and even just under a week past this meeting we are already realizing that we should have had Matt sign a nondisclosure agreement. Although he was a nice, friendly guy, that doesn't stop him from repeating our ideas to other people.

Print shop meeting with Nick Kakish (Tuesday)

Tuesday morning, we met with a family friend who has owned and operated his own print shop for 31 years. He gave us specific advice on the difficulties of competing in such a struggling market. Nick helped to explain the difference between building a product that will sell and building a product that someone desires. This played right into the minimal viable product segment Steve Blank discusses. He also encouraged us to bring printing in-house and outsource the binding; this is the opposite of most business peoples' advice to us so far. This is something that can later be tested for price points customers will want to pay and the time they expect it to take for us to deliver them their product.

Week 1 Test

With so many copyright hindrances and printing issues, it has been difficult to figure out which direction to move, especially regarding prototyping and customer feedback. Because there are only two open-source (outdated) copies of the Bible, the only way we can print a Bible in full is by using one of these versions. The first problem with this is that both versions are waning in popularity. There are still those who choose these versions, but our target market does not fit into the demographic of these readers/buyers.

Our initial hypothesis was to test 10 of our friends and see if they were offered a high-quality ASV Bible at a majorly discounted price whether or not they would switch from reading NIV to ASV. As we began discussing the hypothesis, we noticed immediate holes, mostly centered around this experiment having too many variables. With so many moving parts, it was impossible to isolate any part of the test to receive conclusive data.

Another error we realized was that asking our friends/family is not necessarily helpful because they love us and want to support our ideas. Asking strangers presents the possibility of hearing fresh and new ideas along with honest feedback, which is the most important. Friends and family are more likely to lie to us for the sake of not hurting our feelings if they dislike something versus a stranger who has no problem expressing how they feel about you and your product.

We realized that to run any kind of test we would need to create a prototype that will give a clear understanding of our product (our minimal viable product). The test however was never completed. After calling countless local print shops we knew the copyright infringement rules were scaring people away from helping, even when we mentioned they would be for educational use only. We decided we would spend the time and individually scan each page into our printer, and then find someone to bind our prints. Again, we couldn't find anyone locally to do this for us. The only company that offered gave us a 5 week turnaround and was going to make us pay $180 to have it done in one week's time, so we began learning to do hardback binding as well.

Our hypothesis ultimately shifted to: we can have a simple prototype made quickly and locally. We invalidated that hypothesis very quickly. Through this process, we now have the understanding and experience to put together an MVP that can be used in further experiments. Additionally, we spoke with a few people in Austin, Texas, that offered to show us how to build a professional quality MVP if we drive down to their print shop, so Cooper will be planning a trip there soon.

Week 1 Business Model Canvas

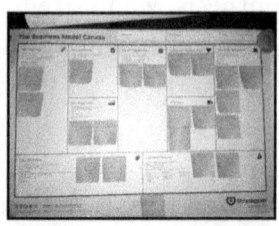

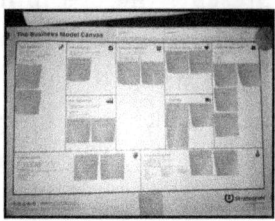

Icarus Aerial Technologies

Week one's value proposition was not received well by the farmers that I talked to. They did not see the value in any near infrared or other analysis about their crops. Some of the issues may have been from the size of the farms because most of the farms at the farmers markets are small to medium size. I would say not more than an acre.

Another issue I ran into was a rejection of anything from the outside. The farmers seem to be suspicious of me when I told them about sensor technologies and UAV use for precision agriculture. I got the distinct feeling that these farmers had their guard up against being sold stuff. I am wondering whether age is also a factor. Most of the farmers were age 50 plus, and seemed to know what they wanted to do when talking about farming techniques.

I approached the subject from different angles based on their responses to my open questions. Each value proposition (environment, pesticide, insecticide) had an answer on their farm.

I also experienced a difficult time explaining the technology to them. It may have been partially my fault because of my lack of detailed knowledge of near infrared technology. It also definitely seems to be a consumer segment that requires education first. Even if I were to get on their farmland, take pictures and show them the data, the real value is the actionable steps from that data. As I've studied near infrared and NVDI the past few weeks, I have found just how complex the data can be.

So, the hypothesis was, "Will farmers see enough value in the infrared data to pay for it?" Out of all the farmers at both farmers markets, zero farmers would allow us to even come out to test our product on their land.

Park Ave

This week the Park Ave team worked on developing our business model using both images and a business model canvas. The first picture you see depicts the Park Ave business model using drawings, while the second is the Park Ave business model using the Business Model Canvas. Additionally, the Park Ave team wanted to test one of our most critical assumptions this week—that homeowners and/or business owners would want to sell their parking in advance and drivers would want to reserve those spots.

Our hypothesis was twofold; first, "Would potential sellers be willing to sell their parking spots a day or so in advance?" and second, "Would people pay money to reserve those parking spots for the next day?" To test this, the Park Ave team decided the best experiment would be to ask businesses and homeowners to allow us to reserve a parking spot and try and sell that parking spot to a stranger, who would pay at arrival to the parking spot.

TEST DESCRIPTION:

In order to test the value chain (money paid for advance parking), the team needed to go into the field and see if a buyer and a seller would commit to it. The team went out to Oklahoma City to see if the value chain would hold during the Big XII Baseball Conference. The test's methodology was as follows: For the first objective, the team sought out people selling parking around the arena where the conference was taking place. The team's goal was to find one seller who would sell their parking to Park Ave in advance for the team to resell. This would confirm the first part of the hypothesis. After this, the team's second objective was to flip that parking spot by selling it to someone who was going to the game the following day. The goal was to find one buyer who would commit to buying parking in advance. This would confirm the second part of the hypothesis, validating the value chain.

RESULTS:

The test only half-validated the team's hypothesis. While a seller did allow us to buy parking in advance, the team could not sell this parking. This is primarily because college baseball games hosted in minor cities are not part of the target market. Since the event was held in a city that already had the parking infrastructure to host major events (ie, OKC Thunder), parking for this event was not an issue. Additionally, the team discovered that we needed a better strategy for convincing buyers. They need to be convinced of the team's credibility up front. The team is still exploring methods of how Park Ave, as a university-based startup, can persuade customers of its legitimacy.

CLASS 3, WEEK 2—VALUE PROP AND INVALIDATED HYPOTHESES

I was very excited for class this week, because it meant I got to hear results from the first round of hypothesis testing! Validated or invalidated hypotheses awaited.

News and announcements

At the end of week 1, students asked if they could give anonymous feedback through a survey. So I put one up on Survey Monkey and shared the link.[15] Most of the Summer Accelerator members responded here.[16]

Class started with news items I wanted to get quickly out of the way, namely: update blogs each week by Monday night, document your interviews and experiments immediately after they happen, run at least one experiment each week (program is built on a weekly cadence), Demo Day page up (http://ouaccelerator.eventbrite.com), mentor relationships (make sure to keep in touch), and legal updates (need to file to get seed money). I was also waiting on the debt contract from the lawyer—this will be a good thing to have done in advance of the Summer Accelerator next time!

---

15 https://www.surveymonkey.com/s/XK9WZ93
16 https://www.surveymonkey.com/results/SM-WFJ8MMP/.

CLASS 3. WEEK 2—VALUE PROP AND INVALIDATED HYPOTHESES

Mentor dinner follow-up

We had a brief recap of the mentor dinner with Elaine Hamm. Officially, Elaine is the director of the Proof of Concept Center at i2e.[17] Even more importantly, she readily offers her unfiltered and unbiased opinion on a startup's potential future. She was exactly what the teams needed at the start of the Summer Accelerator.

I asked the students what they thought about the dinner, and they pointed out Elaine's question, "What do you fear most?" I think this is a really great question, since entrepreneurs are being trained to ignore all warning signs and carry on ahead. The main focus of the Summer Accelerator is to test assumptions methodically and critically, and only by knowing what you fear can you do that. Interestingly, when the teams presented their lessons learned at the end of the ten weeks, Elaine's name kept coming up.

We then started the conversation about the Udacity videos they watched from Steve Blank on **value proposition**. Next week I'm going to start with a presentation of the experiments the teams ran, to close the book on the previous week, before starting the new week's topic.

Conversation and key points on Udacity videos

The class discussed some of the key take-aways they had from the Udacity videos this week. We started with the difference between fact reporting and analysis. Fact reporting looks simply at what happened, in contrast to the deeper understanding that analysis provides by explaining what it means for the business. Many startups think their company is the invention, when in reality it's the *new* business model. Product-market fit means finding paying customers who will be upset

---

17 i2e is a not-for-profit corporation focused on growing innovative small businesses in Oklahoma and making a positive impact on the state's economy. As a Venture Advisor, Elaine supports overall business commercialization efforts, including assisting with market assessments, development of business strategies, evaluation of business plans, competitor analysis, preparation of investor presentations, and facilitating access to the Angel and Venture capital markets. http://www.i2e.org/about/staff/elaine-hamm/

CLASS 3, WEEK 2—VALUE PROP AND INVALIDATED HYPOTHESES

if you go out of business. And last, we discussed value proposition, which means the value the startup is providing to its customers.

The main point we circled around was the difference between a value proposition and a feature. Value props are what are important to your user; features are what deliver the value proposition to the customer. For example, "realtors need better pictures and movies from more angles to better sell their homes" is a value prop, as opposed to "realtors need drones." The key is to not presuppose the solution. With a little practice, we got all of our value props into language a customer would use, which is step 1 towards getting them validated. Value props can only be validated when sold to the customer, and the customer will only buy when they understand the value prop in their own language.

To begin our rework of the canvas, particularly to focus on value prop, each team presented their experiment from the previous week. In each case, the test did not pass. On a side note, I hate using the word failure here, because a failed test is emphatically *not* a failure! In fact, it most likely means you will save time and money by not chasing bad ideas any further.

A few important ideas came up from discussing the tests. One was that even though the test didn't pass, the team wasn't sure if they had gotten good information back. That was purely a test design issue, and I expected the teams would get more adept at designing tests as they went along. I asked what a team would do differently, depending on whether the test comes back yes or no. If the team would do the same thing next, the test wasn't good.[18]

Another idea that came up was the concept of "guardrail to guardrail," borrowed liberally from the book, *Nail It and Scale It*.[19] We had learned in week 1 how to interview customers without leading them down your path, since you're trying to uncover frustrations. While everyone can improve that skill constantly, the issue was the

---

18 See the chapter, **The precommitment mechanism for accountability in the Summer Accelerator,** for more details.
19 http://www.nailthenscale.com/

CLASS 3, WEEK 2—VALUE PROP AND INVALIDATED HYPOTHESES

difference between the customer interview (to uncover frustrations) and an experiment trying to sell something to a customer.

People are pretty good at telling you what they are frustrated with, and they are also pretty good at telling you if they would buy what you are selling. But people are terrible at proposing ideas to solve their own problems that they would then buy once the solution is built! That's the catch, and it's where the entrepreneur does the bulk of the work. An entrepreneur should use customer interviews to learn about problems, come up with a solution that she thinks would solve the customer's problem, and then try to sell the customer the solution. The feedback from the last step, where the customer either says yes (score!) or no (why?) is where all the real learning happens.

Adding in value prop

The teams then went back to the proverbial drawing board to update their canvas with both their learnings from their experiments and the value prop discussion. Already in week 2 I saw a few pivots to chase after better customers and to get people to commit to being beta testers. That was a win in my book! Early adopters are key to any startup's initial growth.

Steve Blank recommends discussing the following ideas:

- Waterfall vs Agile—while Agile operates on a weekly cycle that constantly checks back in with the customer, in Waterfall, all the requirements are gathered up front, and then the team builds the product according to a predetermined plan.

- What's an MVP?—A minimum viable product is a product with the most limited set of a features that you need to generate feedback from a customer.

- Are you assuming the customer problem? or validating? This is the core of the Summer Accelerator's purpose.

- Value Prop vs features—discussed above.

CLASS 3, WEEK 2—VALUE PROP AND INVALIDATED HYPOTHESES

After presenting experiments, discussing value prop, reworking the canvas, and designing new experiments, we didn't get to the first two on the list. The teams decided to discuss Agile in the next startup skills class, so there would be plenty of time for that topic. The point about an MVP being different from a beta is very important, and has come up in side conversations and during office hours.[20] Since I'm so close to the experiments, I feel comfortable that teams understand this idea.

Next startup skills class

This is the list of what I thought the teams might like to do in the startup skills class:

- Practice Scrum and Agile
- Look at different experiments
- Discuss marketing and branding
- Discuss pricing
- Discuss talking to customers more effectively

I put Scrum and Agile at the top because I was hearing that the teams were having trouble deciding what to work on next and how to prioritize tasks. The teams were uncovering lots of assumptions they wanted to work on, and they were also doing a good job identifying the most critical ones. But more work was needed in understanding how to organize a team and completing day-to-day tasks to maintain forward momentum.

---

20 For more on this topic, see the chapter **MVP examples from the real world.**

CLASS 4, WEEK 2—SCRUM, AGILE, AND KANBAN

I got feedback from the students in the class on value prop (Class 3, Week 2) that the teams needed help setting directions and daily to-dos. This is a problem for any company, large or small, and is magnified by the weekly cadence and the sheer level of getting stuff done in the Summer Accelerator. I decided that the **Kanban board**, embodying the two schools of **Scrum** and **Agile**, was the perfect tool to cut through the clutter and focus a team.

Kanban board organization

The heart of the class was the Kanban board[21]—basically, a jumbo-sized to-do list.

The board contains a backlog of user stories, which is in large part the value props and features from the canvas. As teams start work on user stories (which get broken into specific, less-than-four-hour tasks and go in the "To Do" or "Ideas" column), they move the user story into the "In Progress" or "Doing" column.

---

21 To learn more about the Kanban board, this Wikipedia page is a great place to get started— http://en.wikipedia.org/wiki/Kanban_board
22 "Simple-kanban-board," by Jeff.lasovski—Own work. Licensed under Creative Commons Attribution-Share Alike 3.0 via Wikimedia Commons http://commons.wikimedia.org/wiki/File:Simple-kanban-board-.jpg#mediaviewer/File:Simple-kanban-board-.jpg

One of the key aspects of using a Kanban board is to limit the amount of user stories and tasks that go into the "In Progress" column. I think a maximum of two or three is the right number for a two-person team working through weekly iterations. Often a team will get new ideas and want to move them into the "In Progress" column immediately! But that isn't possible: the in-progress tasks/user stories need to get moved into the "Done" or "Completed" column before new ones are launched.

User stories = Lean startup assumptions

In the Lean Startup model, a **user story** is often an assumption that needs to be validated. Therefore, passing or failing the validation test is what moves the user story into the "Completed" column.

 Scrum refers to the concepts of standups and self-governing teams. A **standup** is a daily, short (often ten-minute) meeting in which team members update the group on what they accomplished the previous day, what they have on tap for the current day, and any roadblocks they've encountered to getting their work done. Standups are a great way of removing documentation from the process (although, for my benefit, I'm having the startups document their progress and experiments on their blogs, since I'm not a member of the various teams).

 Self-governing teams means there isn't a manager handing out tasks. Instead, each team member commits to completing certain tasks during the week. Scrum uses the concepts of **sprints** to define the work the team needs to commit to doing in a given period. Sprints of one to three weeks are common. At the end of the sprint, two things happen: (1) the work finished is compared to the work committed to; and (2) the finished work product is demoed for the customer. I've set the sprint time to one week for the purposes of the Summer Accelerator. Startup teams on one-week cadences have excellent momentum. Our experiment process also necessarily demos the work product for the customer each week, too. The demo's purpose is to make sure that what the team is building is what the customer is expecting.

Agile boosts speed and morale

Agile is based on this manifesto: http://agilemanifesto.org/principles.html[23]. It is very software-focused, but, as Joe Justice at WIKISPEED discovered, just change the word "software" to whatever it is that you're working on and Agile still does great! In addition to the proven benefits to workplace productivity, I find it tremendously interesting how Agile appears to dramatically improve team morale and happiness. Taking pride and ownership in one's work and seeing meaningful change over short periods is good for the human spirit!

Putting it all together

The key work we did in class was creating a Kanban board backlog from the canvas. I see these two tools as intricately linked in the weekly workflow. The week starts with an update of the canvas based on the experiments of the previous week. The canvas is fantastic for cataloging the assumptions that need to be worked through and for checking that the business is in line to produce income! But the canvas isn't great at telling a team what to do day to day. That's where the Kanban board comes in. As the team creates the tests and experiments it wants to run, those are crafted as user stories[24] and are added to the backlog. The team burns down the backlog during the week running the experiments, and then the cycle starts over the next week.

Dillon, a member of the Summer Accelerator, taught Agile Product Design at the OU Center for Creation of Economic Wealth during the past semester, and I leaned on his experience to teach this class.[25]

---

23 http://agilemanifesto.org/principles.html
24 Generally in the format of "use feature + to solve problem + result." For more on user stories, see http://www.agilemodeling.com/artifacts/userStory.htm.
25 Our inspiration came from Joe Justice and the WIKISPEED team. WIKISPEED builds cars that get over 100 mpg, all with a distributed team working in a variety of cities and countries around the world, and without any central guidance. As Joe would say, "Awesome!" http://www.wikispeed.org. For a complete write-up of how WIKISPEED uses Scrum, Agile, and Xtreme Manufacuring to achieve its goals, check out the case study I wrote with Martin Kupp from ESCP Europe and Linus Dahlander of ESMT European School of Management and Technology. http://ericmorrow.com/wp-content/uploads/ESMT-813-0139-1.pdf

CLASS 4, WEEK 2—SCRUM, AGILE, AND KANBAN

Class Syllabus for teaching Scrum and Agile

1. Kanban
    a. What a Kanban board looks like
    b. Backlog
    c. User stories (assumptions, features)—use feature + to solve problem + result
    d. Exercise: Transfer business model canvas to a Kanban backlog
2. Scrum
    a. Product owner ranking (HW)
    b. Customer reviews—with rankings and points
    c. Scrum Master (3 biggest impediments)
    d. Sprint/Product iteration
3. Agile Principles—http://agilemanifesto.org/principles.html

ACCELERATOR WEEK 2—TEAM BLOG POSTS

Levaté

Experimenting

Hypothesis: 50 wheelchair users will agree to test a Levaté unit Prototype:

- Ask as many wheelchair users as possible: Would you test Levaté when we have a working unit ready?
- If yes: awesome! We've added you to our list of beta-testers.
- If no: Why not?
- Continue by hitting up contacts, email list, and cold-calling new WCU centers until 50- person goal is attained.
- Evaluation: Get 50 WCU's signed up by the next mentor dinner, 6/4/14.

Findings From Experiment

Promising. After 4 workdays, Levaté LLC has achieved 64% of our target, or 32 wheelchair users signed up to beta-test a Levaté unit. The team believes that the 50-person goal can be achieved by the end of the week of 6/3/14 at the absolute latest.

While not a complete success, the team is well on its way.

Sage Learnings

Levaté LLC has over the course of the past week been surprised by the generally very positive response the device has gotten as the team expands their outreach efforts. Key stakeholders in the wheelchair community now acting as advocates for the LLC include a former and a current Ms. Wheelchair Oklahoma, the President of Ms. Wheelchair California, and the President of Ms. Wheelchair America, the directors of Paralyzed Veterans of America in both Oklahoma and Texas, the directors of accessibility centers across the nation, as well as local therapists.

Said one wheelchair user, "I'm going to be looking for things I haven't been able to do in 18 years."

Additionally, wheelchair users this week identified a key use for Levaté that the LLC had previously not considered as much, that is, to be able to more easily transfer to and from their wheelchair and a surface of differing height, such as the booth at a restaurant or their motor vehicle.

Wheelchair users also identified future products in the Levaté line of products, including an umbrella holder for wheelchairs for use during inclement weather and a grocery cart attachment for use at a store.

Other gems captured from the sign-up survey:

"Thank you for the ingenuity."

"I cannot even reach stuff in my hutch unless I ask my husband. This would give me so much more independence, a normal person just don't know what we go through."

This brings up a great lesson learned for the Levaté LLC team: the difference between customer discovery and customer (or tester) acquisition. The LLC team noted a stark difference in the feedback received when Levaté was offered in the form of a survey designed to test the price versus the survey designed to capture beta-testers.

Obviously, this is due to the fact that the beta-test survey is self-selecting, but also undoubtedly because it asks different questions. The key take-away here: always know what the goal is for your customer outreach.

Driven Analytics

Last week was a busy week, and some big milestones were reached.
1. The founders team met and hashed out the very important matters of who will be investing their prize money and what equity percentages will be, vesting schedules etc. This was a long and messy meeting but was required in order for us to be able to move forward.
2. We filed our provisional patent with the USPTO, which doesn't mean that much besides the fact that we have some hope at getting a patent on certain things at some point in the future.
3. We reincorporated as a Delaware S-Corp. This is the best corporate structure for us and will help when it comes time to try and get funding.
4. We had about a 30-minute teleconference with the Pritzker Group, a VC firm based in Chicago with offices in LA as well. They heard our whole pitch and discussed what they would like to see us get accomplished over the next 1-2 months, as well as where they would like us to be before they would seriously consider funding us.

For week 3 in the Accelerator, I am on vacation so experiments will be limited, but I expect to accomplish the following:
1. Interview 5–10 people who have recently purchased a car to get their feeling on how receptive they would be during the finance part of the purchase to buying another product. Specifically, I will be trying to gauge how defensive people are by that point in the process and try to determine if (A) introducing the product that late in the buying process will

negatively impact adoption rates, and (B) should we not try to sell this to car owners as an added feature but rather sell it to dealerships as a marketing tool for which they fully absorb the cost.

2. Email all of my previous dealer contacts and try to set up 3–4 meetings next week to specifically discuss with them the plan for doing testing of our device with real customers and with the dealership. In the meeting I will be asking for $1000 to cover deploying 5 devices.[26] I think this is a small enough amount to not require much as far as approval is concerned but enough to get them to have real skin involved, which will help with getting good feedback.

Sowers Publishing

Meeting with Mr. McSpadden (Thursday)

Thursday, I went to meet with the only book binder within 100 miles (of Norman, OK) that was willing to work with me. The meeting was extremely rough. Mr. McSpadden, owner and pretty much everything else, was taught by his father in the '40s how to bind books. He took over the family business and is now 74 and close to retirement.

He gave me over two and a half hours of his time to help me understand how in over my head I am and a little about bookbinding too. This was the perfect example of wanting to hear a yes or no, and not maybe; Mr. McSpadden made it clear that bookbinding the correct way, and with the quality Caitlin and I desire, is a dying art. He only knows of 1 other binder that still knows how to do this more than a hobby.

The process is 42 steps long from start to finish and takes 9 to 11 years to grasp, and is only possible through an apprenticeship. Pricing was more than I was hoping for. The cheapest vinyl cover is $44, faux

---

26 For more on this topic, see the chapter, **MVP examples from the real world.**

leather hardback is $49, and genuine leather covering cost $89! That is start to finish in his hands and does not include the shipping to or from, or the gas and time to drive over an hour to his little shop.

As negative as he was, he offered to take on any project we would throw at him with the hopes of returning between 10 and 50 books in 3–5 weeks' time. The material he used was much better quality than our original prototype, and luckily I convinced him to sell me some of the good stuff to continue making our prototypes, as well as pointing me toward Talas.com, where we can purchase additional material. His wife was there and looked at our original prototype and was extremely pleased with the workmanship, while Mr. McSpadden threatened to tear it up if I ever bought crap like that in his shop again! She also was amazed that Caitlin was able to find directions for bookbinding online, which leads me to wonder if I should keep searching new and innovative binding techniques.

He told me that he plans to retire in two years and has no one to take over, which stinks because he has hundreds of books coming in the door every week hoping to get a better binding put on. This could be a cool pivot to hold on to for the future. Additionally, while I was there, he showed me more than 50 brand new Bibles that came in that week that people had bought and sent straight to him to have a quality bind put on. This shows us that there is at least a small market who are unsatisfied with the quality of current Bibles. We ended on a great note, and he is ready for Caitlin to come back in and have her mind blown as well.

Week 2 Test

This week, we hypothesized that customers would like to choose each feature that was added to their Bibles. We created a heat map of 6 options that are widely popular in Bibles today and asked Bible readers to select the 2 most important features and the 2 least important features. On the back of the heat map, we listed 6 features that are hard to find or not available and asked customers if given the option to build their Bible, would they be willing to pay to add these select features, and they could choose as many as they would like.

We thought this test would help validate that customers desire features that are not included in current Bibles, that customers desired to choose the features they purchased, and most importantly, that customers would be willing to pay money for this product. The test was planned to be conducted in Mardel in Norman, but the assistant manager, who is always rude to me (even though I'm their top customer every month), told me I would have to speak with the actual manager come the week of June 2. So Cooper "went shopping" in Barnes & Noble to conduct the experiment where in two and a half hours only 3 people went to the Christian section. The first lady was in a hurry and apologized as she turned us down. The second gentlemen was a middle-aged and was happy to fill the heat map out. Afterwards, he asked what we planned to do with this marketing research, and I told him about MakeABible.com.

Icarus Aerial Technologies

Talking with farmers did not get us anywhere in week two. The guest speaker (Elaine Hamm) at the weekly Accelerator dinner, who was knowledgeable about our industry, said that we might consider another industry first because the farming community and the equipment just wasn't there yet. She instructed us to do a 2x2 matrix to decide which industry would be both the most accessible and the most lucrative.

We listed all of the industries we could think of and plotted them on the matrix. Real estate was one of the most easily accessible and potentially lucrative industries we could find. With this in mind, we pivoted to real estate. Our goal was to get at least one real estate agent who would agree to allow us to take some aerial photographs and video of one of their listings. Then, if we could agree on the quality of the photo/video, ask if they would be willing to use the photo/video to advertise their listing. We did some research on the top real estate agents in the area so that we could start cold calling them.

In the midst of this, we spoke with our mentor. He confirmed to us that the farmers we would encounter at farmers markets are not the type of farmers that would be interested in our services. He said that there are only a few early adopters of this new technology and they work with large companies. He told us we should try to get in touch with some of these types of farmers and gave us a couple of ideas where to look. We immediately started calling farmer co-ops and extension services. These contacts gave us pretty much the same answers. Most of them said they did not use drones and didn't really have a use for them where they were. One co-op manager said that if he knew where drone agriculture was going, he would have his own business already. Most contacts agreed they did not know where precision agriculture was headed.

We began calling real estate agents over the weekend. Two of them said that they would be willing to have us come out and shoot aerial video of one of their listings. One made an appointment. The other said that she didn't have any listings that would be appropriate for this type of photography, but she said she would call us when she did. A couple agents passed us on to some other agents who might be interested. One has not called back, though he said he was looking for a service like this. This week we hope to shoot at least one home.

We did get interest from one farming company today who said that they would be interested in a demonstration of what we want to do with their crop consultants.

Park Ave

THIS WEEK'S CHALLENGE: COMMUTER PARKING.

This week, Park Ave explored the idea of a new pivot. While special events parking is still the more lucrative market, it is hard to test operations—each new event possesses a unique set of environmental variables that make it difficult to see data trends between tests.

Additionally, it is difficult to acquire customers early on with this model. Therefore, the team explored the idea of commuter parking.

With commuter parking, there is no need to wait for an event—we can test right now. We know where the customers are located. Also, it is reasonable to assume that it will be easy to acquire and retain customers through this model because they will be using the service more regularly.

Here is the **hypothesis** we tested: if we go door-to-door (in Norman, OK) pitching Park Ave, we will acquire 10 people who are willing to sign on as initial customers of our company by providing us the information we need to list spots. (sidebar: we went into this test with two sellers and a total of five spots listed with us, one of which is being currently rented.)

TEST DESIGN: At the beginning of the week, we scouted out a 100-house area west of campus that we wanted to test. Before pitching, however, we wanted to try and soften the target. On Friday we distributed print flyers to all of these houses with the goal of creating awareness before we started knocking on doors. On Saturday, the team set out to revisit these 100 houses and see if we could convince anyone to join the Park Ave community.

TEST RESULTS: Out of the 100 houses the team hit, only 21 people came to the door to speak with the team. Out of that 21 people, no one was interested in signing on with our commuter service, the main three reasons being (1) they use the spots during the day, (2) their children are already using the spots, and (3) they needed their roommates' approval. Additionally, several people said that $1 per day is too cheap for parking near campus, citing OKC parking lots that cost $140–$235 for monthly passes. The biggest limiting factor to this test was that, due to extenuating circumstances, only two members of the team could be in town this weekend to perform the test. The team is still discussing about whether this data is enough to properly invalidate the test. The biggest piece of information is that people are not willing to sell commuter spots for cheap; they want three figures to compensate the possible inconvenience. What this means is that this week the team will be looking to either test a higher commuter price or look for a neighborhood farther out that would be worth $1 per day parking.

CLASS 5, WEEK 3—CUSTOMER SEGMENTS AND LEAN STARTUP EXPERIMENTS

Moving into the third week of the Startup Accelerator, I was starting to get more of a rhythm for how the Tuesday morning, Lean Launchpad canvas class, should run.

News and Updates

Funding

To get funding, I needed the teams' Articles of Organization and Certificate of Incorporation, as well as the signed Promissory Note. It took a little while to get the legal issues sorted, and the next iteration of the Summer Accelerator will be able to move faster since the documents are now all available.

Blogs and writing

In addition to writing a weekly blog, I also wanted the teams to start adding daily updates so that I could track their progress and results closer to real time. (This ended up being too big a hurdle and didn't happen.)

Mentor relationships

It seems like the teams aren't making full use of their mentors to open doors and help out with the experiments. However, the experiments

CLASS 5, WEEK 3—CUSTOMER SEGMENTS AND LEAN STARTUP EXPERIMENTS

they are running are really aimed at potential customers, and nothing beats actually talking with the real potential customers (rather than seeking advice from mentors).

Kanban board

I wondered if anyone starting using a Kanban board after the Agile class. There was a mixed reaction, which to me indicates I need to update that syllabus. The main feedback was that they needed more time practicing with it in class. I thought if the teams continued to have trouble planning their daily tasks, then we would revisit Agile again. Multiple touch points are often critical in education!

Books

I learn a lot from books (here are some I recommend[27]). I wanted to know if anyone had time or interest in reading. I asked if they wanted me to assign books to the group as a whole or to recommend books specifically for an individual. The class asked to have a group book to read. I started with *Nail It Then Scale It*,[28] by Nathan Furr. We agreed to discuss the assigned book at the start of each Thursday's startup skills class. Interestingly, I later read *Delivering Happiness*,[29] by Tony Hsieh, and he talks about how he keeps a library of books available for Zappos employees. A good library is a fantastic team learning tool.

Results of Experiments

After updates, we presented the results of the previous week's experiments. Once again, we found that a lot of the tests were not validated. This is to be expected as teams pivot far and fast in order to find product-market fit. Levaté, the wheelchair lift team, was able to validate their experiment from the week. Elaine, from i2e, a nonprofit

---

27 http://www.ericmorrow.com/books
28 http://www.amazon.com/dp/0983723605/?tag=ericmorrow-20
29 http://www.amazon.com/dp/0446576220/?tag=ericmorrow-20

CLASS 5, WEEK 3—CUSTOMER SEGMENTS AND LEAN STARTUP EXPERIMENTS

that invests in high-growth startups in Oklahoma, had offered to fund their prototyping if they could get 50 people to commit to beta-testing the product with them. Levaté had previously tried to presell the lift or take a cash deposit, with limited success. But once they started asking for full contact information and a commitment to use the device during a trial period, sign-ups took off! The team got over 60 sign-ups in the week following Elaine's offer. Here's a link to the sign-up form they used.[30]

Steve Blank Video Discussion

The class watched the Steve Blank video on customer segments. Here are the discussion questions I had prepared:

- What did you get from the video?

- What have you learned about your customer segments?

- Four market types: existing, resegmented, new, and clone

- Different types of segments: users, payers, recommenders

The students focused on the market types and tried to understand what kind of market they were playing in. We also talked about the different segment types, particularly from the perspective of following the money. An easy example is a teenager buying a car—the salesperson knows that the money for the car is coming from the parent, and so she needs to cater to both the interests of the teenager and the interests of the funding source.

The exercise for customer segments, before updating the canvas, was to draw a "Day in the Life of Your Customer." The better the teams understood what their customers are doing and what motivates them, the better they'd be able to create a product or service that will solve their problems or fulfill their needs. The pictures didn't have to be fancy! I'm strictly a stick figure drawer myself. And there wasn't

---

30 http://bit.ly/Xy3bSx

CLASS 5, WEEK 3—CUSTOMER SEGMENTS AND LEAN STARTUP EXPERIMENTS

a set format either. Some teams made boxes, like comics; some used sticky notes; and some drew free-form over a whole page.

My rule for marketing in general is, if I could take away the name of your company and replace your company with a different company, and the marketing would still make sense, then the marketing is too generic. So I challenged all the teams to dig deeper and be very specific about their customer, maybe even choosing one particular customer to follow. Levaté did a good job here, describing in detail a day in the life of Miss Wheelchair Oklahoma. Through the pictures and stories, I got a really good sense of who she is and how she spends her time. Notice that this is not a product pitch—the story shouldn't spell out exactly why the person needs your product! They should be (and already are) living a life independent of what you are developing.

In line with drawing a customer's "Day in the Life" is the need to describe the customer archetype. To me these are two sides of the same coin, and if the team can draw the story, they can flesh out the archetype pretty well. The best way to get to know your customer better is to spend more time with them!

Updating the Business Model Canvas

Each week the teams were responsible for updating their canvas, in particular, the relevant box that they studied that week (through the Udacity videos). The teams have settled on using a jumbo-sized canvas covered in sticky notes. Assumptions that have been tested and invalidated are removed and replaced with new ideas. The canvas stands in for the overall project plan and helps keep the teams focused on making money by selling to customers.

Moving forward

In homage to the "speeding up" aspect of the Summer Accelerator, I asked the teams to run two specific experiments this week. Week 1 and week 2 were to get the teams on the same page regarding the hypothesis-test model, using the canvas to track ideas, and building

CLASS 5, WEEK 3—CUSTOMER SEGMENTS AND LEAN STARTUP EXPERIMENTS

a weekly cadence. Now I wanted the teams to start making more progress faster, with only two months till Demo Day! I wanted them to have validated a real business model with actual customers by the time Demo Day arrives at the end of July. To do that, they needed to be running more tests and talking to more customers, in order to really validate a lot of hypotheses and assumptions.

CLASS 6, WEEK 3—CUSTOMER ACQUISITION

At the start of week 3, I asked the students what obstacles they faced in quickly running experiments and finding paying customers. I wanted to structure the curriculum to be as helpful as possible for their current problems. I believed that that philosophy would bring the classroom learning out of the theoretical and into the practical and relevant. In week 3 the teams asked to discuss customer acquisition.

Where prospective customers come from

We started class by thinking about how you would find "customers" for a language immersion dorm on campus. (On a side note: This is a little project I worked on with Dillon from CCEW.) A language immersion dorm would pair American students learning a foreign language with exchange students to the university who are native speakers of the language. The pairs would live together in university housing and have access to a variety of extracurricular activities, such as movie nights and cooking classes. The housing and events are foreign-language only. The American students would get a great chance to learn and practice the language they are studying, and foreign students would get a chance to live with Americans and get plugged into the local community.

In order to find the American students, we brainstormed that it would be possible to get the emails from the language department for everyone studying the language at the university. It would also be possible to find student clubs that are interested in the language. One could also drop in on language classes in person to pitch the students on the dorm.

In order to find the exchange students, it would make sense to contact the Study Abroad office, which arranged everything related to exchange student life on campus.

Find your audience where they already are

The purpose of the exercise was to think about where your target audience is already aggregated and go after them there. It is much easier to find your audience doing the things they already do (like going to class) than to try to get them to do something out of the ordinary, like come to your website.

Then for each team we considered where their customers were being aggregated. We took a quick detour through soap opera land. Soap operas were originally developed as a way of aggregating stay-at-home moms, the main purchasers of household goods, in order to sell them soap. The first step in trying to reach your customers to sell them things is to figure out where they are.

The teams came up with a variety of responses. Some teams were targeting businesses that want to be found, like car dealers and real estate brokers. Others needed to target groups of people going to special events or wheelchair-related facilities (like a rehab center). Outside of the direct approach route, it was also possible to find your audience through aggregators like magazines or niche websites. Search engine marketing tools allow you to target people on the basis of keywords they use to look for more information, and Facebook lets you target users on the basis of demographic interests.

Once you found your target audience and figured out how to reach them, the next step in the customer acquisition process is to either ask questions to understand frustrations and opportunities or attempt to sell them possible solutions for their problems or needs (for startups who are pre–product/market fit).[31]

---

[31] See again the "guardrail to guardrail" conversation in *Nail It Then Scale It*.

There are a variety of tools that can make tracking this process easier:

Yesware [32] (for one-to-one) and MailChimp[33] (for newsletters) let you see if people are opening your emails and clicking through on your call to action.

Large organizations use tools like Eloqua to track their email campaigns down to the tiniest detail. We looked at a diagram that showed a make-believe flow of email to contacts on a list, and showed possible split tests and follow-ups, depending on the action the recipient took. While none of the teams need to use such a sophisticated system to reach their clients, I thought it was helpful to understand how a large organization looks at testing and grouping email contacts by their responses to emails they receive.

Customer relationship management lets you track leads through the sales cycle until they become customers. Example companies are Salesforce, Onepagecrm, and Highrise.[34]

We briefly discussed the difference between owning a channel (like an email list) vs renting it (like buying ads). Owning is like aggregating a group yourself, and after you've been in business and had some customers, you'll be able to reach out to that aggregate group directly. Renting is paying to get in front of a group that someone else aggregated—essentially, the business model for Google, Facebook, TV, magazines, and blogs.

At the end of class, we planned tests to run during the week, particularly around customer acquisition. I'm a big believer in preselling or getting down-payments on products to test their viability before beginning work on the technical side of making a product.[35] All of the teams were in the process of trying to attract customer interest for their business.

---

32 http://yesware.com/
33 http://mailchimp.com/
34 http://salesforce.com/, http://onepagecrm.com/, http://highrisehq.com/
35 For more on this topic, see the chapter **MVP examples from the real world.**

ACCELERATOR WEEK 3—TEAM BLOG POSTS

Levaté

WELCOME TO OUR NEW WEBSITE!

Hi everyone! Welcome to our new website for Levaté. We hope you enjoy it. Of course, it's a work in progress, so feel free to shoot us an email (levatelift@gmail.com) with any comments, suggestions, or questions you have. This is the first website either of us (Ethan and Dillon) has made, but thankfully SquareSpace, our website building and hosting service, makes the process pretty easy.

Our plan is to use this part of the site (the blog) to post more or less weekly updates on our progress. That should do two things. First, it will show you the progress we're making. Second, it will help keep us accountable! There were three big things we worked on in the past couple weeks: building a prototype in the OU machine shop, attending the endeavor games and networking with wheelchair users, and meeting with i2E in Oklahoma City to initiate the funding process.

In the machine shop

So now, for the exciting part: the prototyping! The bulk of our machine shop work this past week went towards building a rough prototype that had a working pneumatic cylinder. By working, I mean to say that it lifted 200–300 lbs of weight (chair included) a full 12 inches off the ground. Unfortunately the air compressor we're using only reaches about 100 psi, and we need air pressure of about 150 psi for it to lift any substantial weight. This video has more details.[36]

Our next step is to find a compressed air tank that has the required pressure so that we can test it with weight on the chair. Though we certainly had a "blast" welding this prototype together!

Welding the cylinders together!

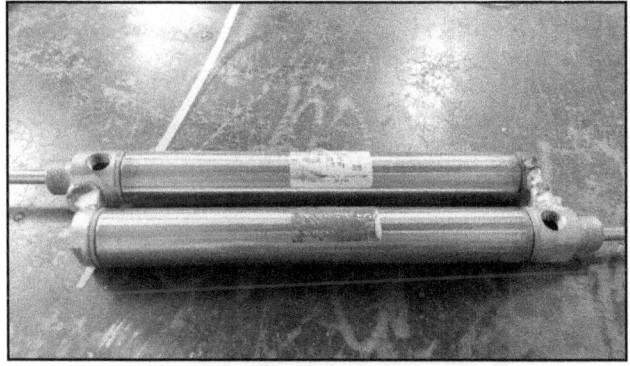

The welded pneumatic cylinders.

---

36 https://www.youtube.com/watch?v=xr8B6mkWaUw

ACCELERATOR WEEK 3—TEAM BLOG POSTS

Surprisingly lightweight—they weigh less than 2 lbs combined. Notice how they actuate in opposite directions to gain double the lift of a single cylinder.

In the next day or two, we'll have more to report on the pneumatic cylinder after we find a suitable compressed air tank. Likely we'll just use a paintball gun–type tank—the kind that's compressed up to 4500 psi or more.

In the meantime, we're also exploring the possibility of using a hydraulic cylinder (hydraulic = liquid, pneumatic = air) powered by a small motor. The advantages of this are that it could potentially lift more weight more easily, while also being easy to recharge. Everyone has a wall outlet, after all, whereas air compressors are less common. We'll have more to report on this in the next couple of days as well— Ethan has been spending many an hour visiting industrial supply shops to find the specific kind of cylinders we need.

Endeavor Games in OKC

We had the opportunity to attend the Endeavor Games on Friday, which Ethan and I loved. Everyone we spoke to there was kind, had a great attitude, and was willing to speak with us for a few minutes as we talked to them about Levaté. A lot of the wheelchair users we spoke with signed up to beta-test the lift, and we also got some great feedback.

For example, we hadn't thought too much about how much clearance Levaté would have to have off the ground when it's undeployed underneath the wheelchair. Jeremy, a canoe paddler aiming for the gold in Brazil, 2016, explained that he will often pop wheelies over small obstacles so that he doesn't have to go around them. For our lift to integrate seamlessly into the routine of someone like Jeremy, we couldn't risk having it clip or hit the ground while the user is performing such a maneuver.

Watching the table tennis matches at the
2014 Endeavor Games, UCO.

The other interesting feedback we heard makes us want to reinvestigate whether or not Levaté could be covered by insurance. It's our understanding that the vast majority of aftermarket accessories for wheelchairs are not insurance reimbursable. We heard from a couple wheelchair users in the past few weeks that they obtained power wheelchairs with lifts via insurance, as their provider judged that they were medically necessary to effectively transfer. Over the next week, I'd like to investigate whether we could make a similar argument: that Levaté could greatly improve the way manual wheelchair users transfer. It may come to naught, but it's a lead we should run down, since obtaining insurance reimbursement would be huge for us.

Funding meeting

Finally, we met with i2E in Oklahoma City to begin the funding process. It's an exciting milestone to have reached the stage where outside investors are considering Levaté! We filled out a reasonable amount of paperwork, and we've done all we can for now. The investment officer at i2E that is managing us as a client will have to pitch us to i2E's investment committee, which is only phase one of a funding process that will take at least 2 months (and likely longer).

Receiving the funding may take a while, but it will help us scale our prototyping so that we can manufacture enough to have a sizable beta-test and collect plenty of feedback and insights into how our product works in the real world.

Where it's all heading

As you can see, it's been a busy past couple weeks! Looking ahead, Ethan and I have quite a bit of work to do to move the prototyping forward. Right now, we're focusing on getting a working pneumatic or hydraulic cylinder. Then we'll move on to the other components of Levaté.

I also want to chase that insurance question down—that is, whether or not there is a decent chance that the lift could be insurance reimbursable under certain circumstances.

Hopefully you've enjoyed the look into what the Levaté team is working on! As always, feel free to contact us (levatelift@gmail.com) with any questions or comments.

Ethan and Dillon

Driven Analytics

This week's theme: Hofstadter's Law—"It always takes longer than you expect, even when you take into account Hofstadter's Law."

Monday: 6/9/2014

The first three weeks of the Accelerator (vroom vroom) got off to a weak start due to previous conflicts and complications related to our formation. But week 4 is here and it is going to be EPIC!!!

Last week's experiments have further led me to believe that selling the device to customers at the time of purchase is likely to be more difficult than expected, due to the number of objections and the defensiveness that customers seem to have once they get to the finance department. Those results are leading me to begin experimenting with the idea of selling SmartDrive primarily as a marketing tool for dealerships, where they absorb 100% of the cost of the device. This will no doubt change the ad revenue part of the business plan, but how is yet to be determined. One plausible scenario is that a dealer could advertise to devices they have installed for free in perpetuity but they would pay to advertise on devices that they did not install. Perhaps we could charge more for these ads and recover some of the lost ad revenue. This type of change needs to be discussed with the Driven Analytics leadership team and tested in a dealership environment before we could really consider making a change like that.

On that note...This week's experiments will be trying to get money from two dealerships to participate in early-stage device testing. I will meet with two dealerships and give them an update on our progress and ask them to participate in early-stage testing of 10 devices at their dealership. They will be asked to pay $300 per device, for a total of $3,000 each. If they are not willing to participate yet, then I will try to get information about why not and what we would have to do to get them to participate. Is the price too high or is the product offering not firm enough, etc. A lot more thought needs to go into what this testing will involve, so updates will be forthcoming.

Sowers Publishing

Week 3

Mentor Dinner With Adele Beasley (Wednesday)

Adele was a really great fit because of her social entrepreneurial vision. I loved getting to hear about how she has incorporated social entrepreneurship into the structure of her business because that is something that Caitlin and I know is going to be important for our business moving forward. Looking at purchasing statistics for our generation has shown that people are more apt to buy products from companies whose focus is not profit driven, and when deciding between two companies, they will be more likely to purchase from the company with a social focus. Because we are focusing so heavily on college students, we want our social purpose to be a large part of our marketing strategy. We want our customers to partner with us in taking the gospel to the world, and our product allows them to be a part of that purpose, even if they don't have the ability to travel around the world themselves. Adele sounds like she has the same heart to want her customers to partner with her mission.

Having pitching feedback was helpful because we haven't gotten too much on that yet. I know I am not the best at presenting, and I can get carried away on a topic and easily forget about others, so knowing I need to focus on the ending of the pitch is good. One of the more encouraging things was that her first response was agreement that there is a need in the market for improvement. Though I believe there is, and whether there is or isn't, it is good to know that the pitch was enough to describe a convincing need for our product.

Prototype building (Thursday and Friday)

Knowing that we are on a budget, we made a simple solution for producing prototypes. Instead of printing a 1400-page book, we printed 4 books of the New Testament and bound each of them separately. Each of them had a different layout of journal pages, so that we can get feedback and maybe move to cut one out or only produce one type to save time and money. The printing, binding, and time between took roughly 6 hours to complete all 4 copies. Looking forward, I think we can make one no faster than 4 hours but produce a bundle of 10 in less than 10 hours. We need to build our prototypes to accomplish a specific goal, so our goals will need to be set in order to move forward with additional prototype production.

Labor learning curve: We hired 2 people to work 10 hours each week in hopes of speeding up production time.

Weekend on the road

This week had multiple purposes:
1. Vacation with family
2. Time with Kaleo boys
3. Pitch idea to both Bible readers and nonreaders (potential investors)
4. Sold prototypes (4 @ $20) (received payment for 2 of 4)
5. Setup feedback for future (4 prototypes, 2 male and 2 female, 1 gospel in each, feedback from 8 guys and 8 girls in 2 weeks)

TEST & EXPECTED RESULTS

Week 3 test

1. I can sell a bound copy of the gospels for $20. (1 of 5 is success) (100 is success)

Test: In Alabama, I showed the 4 copies of the prototypes to my Kaleo boys and asked if they would pay $20 for each of them. 3 of them bought them, and 2 gave me money on the spot. One of those plus one more planned to take the 2 "girly" Bibles and sell them to girls at Kaleo.

Results: We were not able to sell 100 (we only had time to make 4), so the test is not validated, but will need to be continued after additional prototypes are made. Additionally, we can use this to get feedback from more than just the 4 buyers, but ask them to let others use the Bibles and get feedback on the products from each of them.

2. Pastors will purchase Bibles with journal pages (2 of 5 is success) (50+ is success)

ACCELERATOR WEEK 3—TEAM BLOG POSTS

Week 3 Business Model Canvas

Week 3 Kanban Board

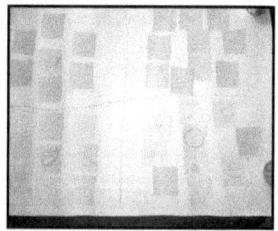

Week 3 Day in the Life of a Customer

Icarus Aerial Technologies

This week we focused all our efforts on real estate. Our hypothesis was that real estate agents would find value in aerial photography and videography for their listings. Our test was to email or call 100 real estate agents. If one of them allowed us to come out and photograph one of their listings and agreed to use that photograph (if we could agree that the quality was good enough), then that was a successful "pass." Otherwise, it was a fail.

We reached out to over 100 real estate agents using cold calls and MailChimp. We also set up a CRM to help us start to manage our clients. The reports were encouraging. We had over 40% open rate (the industry standard is 18%) and over a 4% click rate (the industry standard is 2.8%).

We were contacted by 2 real estate agents. One agreed to allow us to come film. We are awaiting a reply from the other. Our cold calls netted two real estate agents who were very interested. One is out of town at the moment, but the other is helping us set up a filming date as this post is being written. The first part of our test succeeded, but we need to see if the real estate agents will continue to be interested as we ask them to use our services. On the product side of things, we have been told multiple times by real estate agents that they need high-quality photos. A couple real estate agents have tried to use aerial photography before, but were turned off by the low quality. We will need to be selective about which camera we use to gather our media.

Park Ave

This past week, Park Ave faced two tests, the loss of a team member and a pivot. While the results of the past week are not necessarily encouraging, the new direction that the Park Ave team is exploring is an exciting change of pace that may lead the venture down a more promising path.

The Tests, and the Resounding Truth

There were two tests that we laid out this past week: both tested the willingness of people to sell spots with our application. The first test focused on businesses, the second on homeowners. The tests were both designed to acquire early customers and convince these sellers to commit to us.

The first test happened on Thursday. The team talked to 20 businesses on the east of campus (previous research indicates that very few businesses sell parking west of campus). The answer the team heard was ubiquitous: no. We are still in the process of following up with a few of these businesses, but no one jumped out of their seat and said, "I want this!" The first test shook our confidence; between Oklahoma City, Norman commuters, and Norman businesses, no one was stepping forward with extreme interest. The bubble in which this technology was developed last semester began to pop.

The second test, which was scheduled for Monday of this week, did not happen; we were sidetracked by the resignation of one of our team members. He felt that he needed to focus on graduate school applications and his research internship that is about to begin. His reasoning is valid, and we will miss him, but it threw a chink in our plans for the day. That was where the team found itself Monday of this week: discouraged by three weeks of "no" and the loss of a team member.

And then, the idea for a pivot formulated. Boomer Sooner! The Park Ave team wants to take the iPhone application back to the university. We are in the process of scheduling a meeting with the director of the Office of Parking. We want to see if we can find a strong enough problem in OU's parking systems that would justify an application.

The downside to this approach, which was pointed out to us by a guest at dinner last night, is that the value add is less clear and the market is much smaller. However, the team would rather successfully enter a small market to begin with than be stuck on the outside looking in on larger markets. Success with OU would simplify the business challenges of Park Ave: with OU on board, we no longer need to focus on acquiring sellers. We only need to get buyers, and we can reach those buyers through OU-branded sales channels (which are much more trusted than our personal email accounts!), increasing the chance that we will begin acquiring customers and operating like a proper business.

MVP EXAMPLES FROM THE REAL WORLD

I get asked all the time, what are some MVP examples (or experiments) that I can get inspiration from?

What's an MVP?

First and foremost, the biggest problem I see when developing an MVP is that MVP gets confused with beta.

A *beta* product is an early release of your product, designed so customers can play with it and the business can see what happens, get feedback, etc.

An *MVP* is an experiential prototype the business uses to answer a specific question or to get data on a hypothesis. After the first few rounds of testing, the MVP might become a beta. But I often see people's first instinct is to create the beta of their product right away, and I think they would be better served by going with a true MVP to start.

MVP Example #1—Experiential prototyping

Here's an image Levaté had on the front page of their website (http://www.levatelift.com/):

What you're looking at is a quintessential beta product. It looks, acts, and feels much like the final product will look, act, and feel.

To get to this point, though, the Levaté team used human-centered design and Agile production principles to run a series of experiments, or MVPs. One thing the engineering team wanted to know was whether a wheelchair user preferred to be lifted up from the seat of the wheelchair or to have the entire wheelchair itself be lifted, passenger included.

The MVPs they used to test this question looked nothing like this product. In the first test, the team placed stacks of paper underneath the butt of the wheelchair user, lifting that person up from the seat. The team found out that the users did not like the sensation of being far from the wheels, which they tend to grip for support and balance.

In the second test, the team lifted the entire wheelchair up onto wooden pallets, to replicate the experience of being off the ground but still in the wheelchair. The users reported they preferred this feeling, but only up to a maximum height of 12 inches.

Teams using experiential prototyping to test hypotheses can move much more quickly than teams building fully functioning betas. That allows the MVP teams to figure out what customers or users want faster and better. It's also essential to be able to stick to Agile, week-long iterative sprints.

MVP Example #2—The smoke test

One of the first questions any new product or service faces is, does anyone even want this? In other words, is it worth the time, money, and effort it'll take to develop this service? An auxiliary question is, does a customer or user want this product or service in the form that the business is imagining?

Most businesses try to solve this problem with the *Build It and They Will Come* strategy. The business rationalizes the solution in a boardroom, removed from any contact with real customers. They are often shocked to find out that what they imagined as a perfect solution isn't well received in the real world.

The best solution is to use a smoke test, or presale. A smoke test uses a tool like Unbounce.com to build a variety of landing pages that then have paid web traffic directed at them. The goal is to see if anyone signs up to buy something. It is very similar to Kickstarter, where businesses try to raise money for projects they want to work on.

Both are doing the same thing—verifying that there is customer demand or interest in a product before building it.

Another variant on this is the cold call/email. Here you are making a pitch to a potential customer by phone or email and measuring the response rate. One of my summer startup teams, Project Xip, used this methodology when they were ready to make a potential pivot away from their marketplace parking app, in which private sellers of parking spots could find buyers. They couldn't find anyone who was interested in using this app, so they thought about another application in the parking space that would measure the usage of university parking lots. They ran the test by sending cold emails to 20 email addresses of parking directors at universities within a day's driving distance of OU. And within 2 hours they had a 50% response rate. That's enough to validate the idea that there is sufficient interest in the product to continue moving forward. (Note: the product had not yet been built at this moment in time.)

A similar tactic that works well for existing businesses is to ask customers to pay for feature enhancements they want to prioritize. So all feature requests come into a central repository, and the development team works on them in the priority the company deems best. But any feature can be bumped to the top of the line if the user is willing to pay for it. This system quickly highlights which features the user really cares about and which ones are just nice to have.

Levaté used this preorder system to build a landing page form on Google Drive and take signups for beta users. Within a few weeks of opening the form, they had already collected over 150 interested users, complete with contact info. This is a strong indication that there is customer interest in the product. Not quite the gold standard of Kickstarter, but pretty close.

MVP Example #3—The paid pilot

Driven Analytics is another business going through the Accelerator this summer. They plan on using a physical device that plugs into the dashboard to track car usage data. The device has GPS and a cell phone/data connection. They want to sell this product as a service to car dealerships to help with customer satisfaction and retention.

Driven Analytics really needs to test two things at this stage of its development: will businesses pay for any of its proposed features, and what should those features look like? The best MVP for this is the paid pilot.

For Driven Analytics, a paid pilot means getting a car dealership to pay a meaningful amount of money to test out the devices and the data they produce over a specified period. As it turns out, two dealerships signed up within the first week of pitching them! That answers the "will anyone pay for this" question in the affirmative. Now comes the task of trying to figure out exactly what the dealerships need from the device and how they would use the data it collects. Suffice to say, within the first week of selling the device and its benefits, the value prop of the business has changed pretty dramatically, as actually selling a pilot gets a startup business very valuable feedback.

MVP Example #4—Little bets

Another common question I get is, how do you start using Lean Startup or experiential prototyping today? It's all well and good to talk about it in a classroom, but people want practical tips for translating that into real work.

I've borrowed the name of this section from Peter Sims' excellent book, *Little Bets*.[37] And the Mine Fellows in Tulsa, OK, recently applied its principles in a project for United Way[38]. The challenge was to bring new people and projects into the social entrepreneurial ecosystem in Tulsa. The United Way had a special pot of money

---

37 http://www.amazon.com//dp/B0043RSJTU/?tag=ericmorrow-20
38 http://theminetulsa.com/the-mine-final-presentations/

called the New Venture Grant that was earmarked for exciting new initiatives. But it was only the existing nonprofits that were applying for its funding.

The Fellows first came up with the idea of having a pitch competition for the money and giving the cash away in large blocks to the best ideas. But this begs the question, where will new entrepreneurs come from and how will they get prepared to use the cash? And even more importantly, how will the United Way check for quality in the projects? In short, this is a very typical launch project in which there is a lot of risk and uncertainty.

I proposed that rather than creating an elaborate system of checking in on the new entrepreneurs to see if they were using their cash appropriately, and also instead of giving away large chunks of cash all at once, that the pitch competition should be stripped way down so as to only give away a small amount of money—say, $1,000. And rather than giving away $100,000 to two or three projects, at first $10,000 to $20,000 could be given away in $1,000 increments. The recipients would then have 3 to 6 months to do something with the money. I think of that "something" as a Lean Startup–style experiment. After the time went by, the entrepreneurs would come back to the Fellows, discuss what they accomplished, and then be considered for a bigger grant.

And that is the essence of little bets. Rather than placing a few big bets on some very risky propositions, it is better to start with lots of little bets, and then double down on the ones that seem to be working. This methodology would work well in any enterprise. If there's a challenging problem, full of risk and uncertainty, the best bet is to let a lot of different people and ideas have a run at it. If you keep the experiments small—low in capital and short in duration—then the risk of a huge failure goes way down. And when the results of all those tests come back, the company can use data instead of assumptions to decide where to continue investing in innovation.

CLASS 7, WEEK 4—CUSTOMER CHANNELS

Moving into week 4, the teams were one third of the way through their time to build. Week ten, July 23, was Demo Day! To match the urgency and the nature of the Accelerator, I asked each team to commit to completing two experiments this week.

Tests need to be completed in the allotted cycle time

After we went through the normal news items (feedback on mentors, books to read, new places to get dinner, etc), each team presented the results of their experiments. A recurring issue we had in week 4 was that the teams bit off more than they could chew, such that no clear results or learnings could be had from their experiments. The solution to this problem was to only schedule experiments that a team could actually achieve in one week (the cadence I chose for the Accelerator)!

Here are some examples. One team wanted to approach a possible funding source as a test to see if their idea was advanced enough to receive an investment to spur development of functional prototypes. They set up their test to pass if the funder, Elaine Hamm, at i2e, would agree and commit to presenting their business to the board. This is a great test, because it shows both a serious commitment from a potential funder and is something that can be completed in a week.

Another team wanted real estate agents to invite them out to have their properties videotaped by drones, and to have the video posted to the real estate agent's website. However, the team only got verbal commitments from the real estate agents, and the agents didn't get around to inviting them out. Technically, this test failed. But the team is hoping that the agents will invite them out the following week, so we didn't actually learn anything. A better test here would have been to get commitments from agents as step 1, validating that the agents see a need for this service. Then a follow-up test could have been to see how many of the agents that commit invited the team out during the following week.

Now that the teams were in the thick of validating their ideas, I felt like we were starting to slip towards running tests for the sake of running tests, just to see what happens. The purpose of an experiment is to validate (or invalidate) a hypothesis. And the hypothesis should be tied to an assumption on the business model canvas—hopefully, the most critical assumption.

Negative feedback leading to pivots

Even as the teams start to pick up the pace and sell their products to get feedback from their customers, Steve Blank warns of the trough of despair that comes from the need to pivot based on negative or lukewarm feedback. Teams may find that their original idea wasn't as good as they had originally thought. My opinion is this is more a cause for celebration! Rather than wasting another 1 to 2 years of one's life and who knows how many resources, teams can commit to shutting down one option and pursuing another that may turn out to be more lucrative and have more impact.

This is a revisit of the search versus execution concept. The more side paths you can visit, or the more swings of the bat you can take, the more likely you are to find the one idea that gets traction. While in search modes, startups (or young companies) need to be spending their efforts on finding product-market fit. Once that happens, they can then start switching to execution mode.

Getting your product to your customers

The heart of the curriculum in week 4 was distribution channels, that is, the way customers are going to get their products or services delivered. We had a brief rundown of the types of channels available, primarily direct, indirect, and OEM. I encourage startups that are looking for product-market fit to start with direct channels because doing so comes with the added benefit of getting direct customer feedback.

Direct is when the company finds and sells to customers without an intermediary. For example, Icarus planned on calling construction companies themselves to start a conversation and sell photography services. Indirect is when the company works with a third party to get to a customer. For example, Levaté planned to work with wheelchair supply companies to sell their lift to wheelchair users. OEM is when another company buys your product for inclusion in their product that is sold to a customer. Driven Analytics considered this option for their SmartDrive device to be included in a car when the dealer sold it to a customer.

It is important for the startup to know how their customers will get their products. While there may eventually be many ways (you can rent a movie from Netflix, stream it on Amazon, or go to Redbox to pick it up) or channels to choose from, a startup serves its interests well to validate one channel at a time.

Many startups avoid indirect channels because they feel that they are giving away money that belongs to them. However, indirect can dramatically reduce selling costs. For example, the wheelchair team is wondering if it would be better to sell their device directly to consumers or use well-known wheelchair shops. While the advantages of direct sales are straightforward, building out your own sales channel and making sure you get enough traffic involve substantial costs in and of themselves.

First step in the sales cycle

The first step in building a startup is to get traction, that is, to get to the point where people are interested in what you are creating and will make a commitment to your young company. A step you need to take shortly thereafter is to figure out if you can make money selling your product or service. And a big question for channels is cost per acquisition, or how much will it cost to get a new customer in the channel you've selected.

There are many charts available on the web that depict a generic sales cycle, such as this one. [39]

I prefer to use the marketing funnel, as you can see from the whiteboard illustration. It demonstrates how a person becomes a lead and then a client. Layered on top of that is Steve Blank's idea to demonstrate understanding through drawing. By that he means that if someone can draw out an explanation—for example, what their client is doing at every stage of the funnel—then they understand their client well. Here's what the Project Xip came up with.

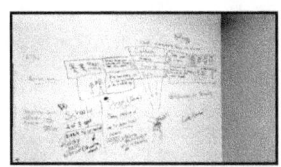

In short, the sales cycle describes everything that needs to happen to find leads and convert them into customers. It tends to fall into categories such as initial contact, first meeting, follow-up, and sale. After a lead becomes a customer, the sales cycle may continue with referrals, upsells, and future purchases, but it is not crucial to work out these elements at this stage of the game.

Here are some key questions to consider when thinking about a sales cycle or marketing funnel:

---

39   http://www.precallpro.com/Portals/31181/images/Identifying The Sales Cycles-resized-600.gif

CLASS 7, WEEK 4—CUSTOMER CHANNELS

How long will it take to get a new lead to become a customer?

What's the lifetime value of a customer? (This affects how much you can pay to acquire them.)

How do you prove a channel? (Prototype it! Get real intent to purchase.)

After building out our sales cycles and drawing them, each team decided on which distribution channel they would focus on first.

Creating new experiments

Class closed as usual with the teams working on their new experiments for the coming week. For week 4, they again needed to have two experiments to work on. Going into week 5, I challenged them to up their velocity and try to get three experiments in per week for the second half of the Accelerator.

CLASS 8, WEEK 4—PITCHING!

In week 4, the teams asked to go over their pitches for the startup skills class. My major teaching point for pitches is that they should do the following:

- include as much *data* from the team's experiments at possible (facts being more interesting than guesses),
- embed *stories* so there is a narrative and flow to the pitch,
- skip *cliches* (if we get 1% of the households in America to buy this), and above all,
- *use images*, not words!

Bundled up in all of that was the need to practice and iterate. I also asked the teams to take notes on the questions they are getting after their pitches at the weekly dinner, and if they heard the same thing more than once, to consider making a change to their pitch.

One topic that came up very quickly is whether they needed to follow a specific format for their presentations. For example, there is the ten slides rule,[40] which I think is helpful. My advice was to be aware of this rule but not to obey it compulsively. Yes, most people listening to your pitch will want to know what the problem is and how you're going to solve it and make money. But telling your story in a compelling way should trump all other considerations.

---

40 http://blog.guykawasaki.com/2005/12/the_102030_rule.html

CLASS 8, WEEK 4—PITCHING!

Text will kill your presentation

The corollary to telling a good story is to *not* use lots of text in your slides. If you do use text, people will start reading off your slide rather than paying attention to what you are saying. That's because people can read faster than you can talk. Slides should be used to embellish your story and provide a visual narrative with tools such as pictures, charts, and graphs.

Overall, halfway through the Accelerator, the teams' pitches were fairly rough. I'm glad we got started on officially iterating them early on. I had originally planned on approaching pitching in week 8 of 10, to prepare for the rehearsal dinner in week 9 and Demo Day in week 10.

Exercises for pitching

I had each team pitch, and then I solicited comments from the group. I was very pleased with the level of engagement and feedback. I had originally planned to have the teams pitch, get feedback, iterate on the spot, and pitch again. But the feedback sessions were very detailed, and we ran out of time! However, the teams already pitch their ideas multiple times a week in class and at the Accelerator dinner (and many more outside of scheduled times), so there would be plenty of chances to practice and improve.

ACCELERATOR WEEK 4—TEAM BLOG POSTS

Levaté

UP NEXT: PROTOTYPES, INSURANCE, AND WEB TRAFFIC

At the Sooner Launch Pad Accelerator, we're operating on "sprints" or iterations of 1 week. In other words, each week we choose 1–3 hypotheses about our business that we want to test.

Here are the three that Levaté is working on over the next week:

1. Can we build a Levaté prototype unit that a wheelchair user could use in their day-to-day life? That includes being portable and having a self-contained air supply, achieving a full 12-inch lift, and being able to deploy/undeploy completely.
2. Could Levaté be reimbursed by insurance under any circumstance? We'll be testing it by interviewing at least 5 decision makers in the insurance industry. If anyone has a connection to Medicare, a private insurance company, or a friend who's been reimbursed for a power wheelchair with lift, that would be a big help for us!
3. Are online ads through Facebook and Google effective ways to raise awareness of Levaté and drive traffic to this website? We'll be meeting later today with Eric Morrow to talk about the specifics of digital marketing and how this could apply to Levaté. Should be informative!

That's what we'll be up to for the next week. Stay tuned for the results of our work!

Driven Analytics

Here goes another week! Last week was great as we won 2 dealership customers and two individuals committed to pay $100 to have devices installed on their cars! At this point, the focus needs to turn to working closely with the two committed dealerships, beginning to experiment with how to create value for them. I do have a meeting on Tuesday with a dealership, who has a new service manager, and last time we met was paying for 2 years of free service for every new car buyer out of the dealership's marketing budget. This meeting will be aimed at establishing a relationship with the new manager and discussing what we are doing. Since we have two dealerships already, I will couch the "ask" a little differently, saying that if they are interested in being involved in this early-stage testing, we are offering a 6-month test program for 10 vehicles at $130 per vehicle.

In addition to the experiments this week, we need to finalize the formation of Driven Analytics, Inc., by getting stockholder agreements reviewed and signed etc. We have a tentative signing meeting for Friday evening, which should allow us to get everything submitted to the OU foundation before July 1st.

Experiments This Week:

1. **Hypothesis**: Floor plan companies want to save money and time for auditing

    Test: Meet with a floor plan company and ask them to try a test on a small dealership. We would charge a set-up fee of $100 per vehicle, but would provide data for free.

UPDATE:

The results of this experiment were neither proven nor disproven. I successfully had a face-to-face meeting with the manager of the Oklahoma City office of a national floor plan company that specializes in dealerships selling sub $15K vehicles. The meeting with her went very well, and she showed great interest in what we might be able to offer. Some key insights included the following:

They audit dealerships twice a month, and they spend a large amount of their auditing time searching for vehicles that the dealerships "doesn't know where they are" or "they are on a customer test drive again." Because many times, dealership cars are at auctions or with the mechanic, and they have a hard timing knowing if they are being lied to or if the car has in fact been sold but the money hasn't been paid back yet.

This type of device would save them a lot of time. They would also like to know if there were any major engine problems, as that could impact the value of the car.

They are likely to be more interested in having a pool of devices that they can deploy at their own convenience based on the risk of a particular dealership, and they would be charged a fee for every time they put it on a new car.

The average turnover of vehicles that they have right now is 65 days, so if devices are staying on cars for 65 days, then there would be the chance to get revenue from it 5–6 times a year.

We discussed different types of pricing structures, and she agreed to take the idea up to corporate, who would have to be involved in a decision to do a test. I owe her some "marketing" materials that she can use to present to the corporate office.

PASS: Yes, we would value

1a. If you would value it, what would your per car discount be for dealerships?
RESULT: NOT ENOUGH DATA
2. Hypothesis: Dealerships that make frequent spot deliveries or have employees driving demo vehicles would pay per vehicle to

know where vehicles are being driven by employees or where spot deliveries are until the financing goes through and they have the money secured.

Test: Discuss spot deliveries and demo vehicles with at least two dealerships and ask if they want to test a device for either $50 for two weeks.

PASS: They commit to doing a test

UPDATE:

This experiment proved to be a non-starter mainly due to the timing. Last week was the end of the month and dealerships are doing everything they can to get in final sales etc. That was exacerbated by the coming 4th of July automotive extravaganza that just about every dealership is gearing up for.

Sowers Publishing

— Types of prototypes moving forward: types, costs, time, purpose for each one.
— Opened bank account
— Customer channels:

BEGIN BUILDING & ADD TO KANBAN BOARD

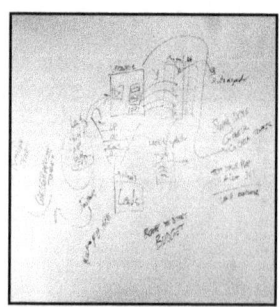

1. Find leads
   — Geographic Target (Look to Barna Group research)

- Facebook
- SM?
- NP?
- GA?
2. Unbounce (Consider using Squarespace for Unbounce page to check traffic?)
    - Video
    - Explanation
    - Click to Buy
3. MailChimp
    - Use autoresponder
    - Send updates

Class Pitch (Thursday)

Feedback:
- Better explanation of certain details, especially main points.
- Too much on problem (2nd time to hear this!)
- Add continuity throughout slides with logo or name
- Match points with points...
- "Red letter" pictures to highlight...
- Problem "we have had" and not "our customers are having."
- Add pictures of problems! (Heavy backpacks kids will have to carry, ink bleeding through the pages, no room for taking notes.)
- Use animation to follow along with speech.
- Explain and show prototype (do not pass around).
- Show or add time-lapse of crappy Bible falling apart.
- Bigger text!
- "OUR RESEARCH! OUR RESEARCH! OUR RESEARCH!"

Meeting with Adam Starling & Staff (Friday)

I was able to sit down with my pastor and 6 staff members for the church to pitch Sowers on Friday afternoon. His feedback was surprising. He said that he doesn't use his print Bible anymore and doesn't even know where it is! He uses his iPad and the YouVersion app. He preps his studies with that and types them out on Microsoft Word. He also wanted me to restate my value proposition so that he could fully understand why someone would chose to buy a Sowers Bible over the current Bibles offered.

Adam is very cut and dry, so he told me that I was asking for details from the wrong person, and then offered to put me in contact with the local pastors he knows and a few other people that might be able to give more valuable feedback. He made sure that I knew Sundays would be a bad time to contact pastors and most likely not a good time to speak with people about buying a product as well. He told me that Sunday at church is a time for people to get away from the consumer market and connect with family without distraction and that Sundays are the busiest day for pastors.

Lastly, I was able to explain the social side of Sowers in hopes that he would understand the heart and vision we have. He thought that being a nonprofit could be an easy way to market this, and not truly give up a large portion of the proceeds. He made sure that if we were solely a social venture that we limit the reach we try to have and hone in on what we truly care about. That will be something Caitlin and I will have to discuss later this summer.

The staff members in the room gave me much easier to hear feedback, though most likely not as helpful. 6 of the 6 said they would buy this product and undoubtedly prefer printed text to e-reader. Because they themselves read the Bible so often and take notes while doing so, they wanted to know about having pages you can take out and add back in. This is not the first time I have heard this! So I will need to brainstorm that one. Besides that, the staff was extremely excited and wanted to know how soon it would be up and running.

Outsource contacting (Friday)

After speaking with the men at Suburban Graphics on Thursday, I began to worry about the reality of actually getting these Bibles produced. Hearing from multiple printing shops that we need to bring the printing in-house, I started researching companies that sell the printing and binding machinery that we would need to produce our products. This was extremely frustrating for multiple reasons. First, the majority of these companies are located in either India or China. It took me hours to find a company located in the U.S. Second, no one lists the price of their machines online because the market is both competitive and one-to-one selling focused.

So I reached out to 6 companies located in Europe and Asia, and 2 in the U.S., asking each for product information on their line of products and price estimates. The responses were overwhelming. Not only do I not know the product specifications many of them need to pair me with the correct machines, but many of the machines that I was given prices for were well over $100,000. This is not even the printing presses, only the binding equipment. The printing/binding industry reminds me of the airplane industry because many of the used machines that are still over $150,000 are from the 1970s, '80s, '90s and early 2000s. Overseas machines are much cheaper than domestic; however, I did not look into the cost to ship them to the U.S., load them on a truck to Oklahoma, and have them set up here. Not to mention, if something goes wrong, contacting the manufacturer would be very costly and time consuming. On the other side, U.S. made machines are more than twice the cost of the foreign competitor, but will not require overseas shipping and will be much easier to contact for machine maintenance and repairs in the future.

This information was very much a pain to obtain, but will be useful for investor pitches soon.

Icarus Aerial Technologies

This week we set out with our first responses from our last round of hypothesis testing. Three companies are interested in our services at some level. One company in particular has asked for us to compose a price structure for them as well as a noncompete agreement. This is to keep us from competing with the other builders in the same area, giving them the advantage in selling their listings. We immediately began strategizing about what price structure we would like to employ. Casey has begun composing noncompete drafts so we can present them with our pricing and paperwork this week. The company is interested in aerial photography as a marketing tool, replacing the blueprints that they use now. They value for them is the ability to show relevant photos from above to interested buyers. They can point out the particular house the client is interested in and show the context of the rest of the neighborhood and surrounding amenities. The client is also interested in using drone videography to show their listings on their website.

It seems as if builders are the more interested clientele on the whole. They have more real estate to show and multiple phases of that real estate being built. Builders have larger buildings and a larger context in which to show those buildings. Not as many services exist for developers to show not only their individual houses but also the other aspects of the real estate they have developed, like the pool houses, club houses, walking tracks, fountains, water features and other things. These are important features that help highlight the benefits of choosing to live in a certain neighborhood.

We are still reaching out to more real estate developers this week. We also have called developers. We also set out to call 10 construction companies this week. Construction companies are another opportunity that we see for our services. We have not had much response, but we might need to try more companies. We also need to wait a few more days for responses to come.

Much of this week was spent on the product end of the spectrum. Not much time had been spent on our product outside of flying the Phantom for the last month and a half. I spent several days researching exactly which type of drone to purchase and which type of camera to go with it. Our money came in yesterday, which means we need to buy our product in the next day or so. It has been a very difficult line to walk. Drones come in all shapes and sizes. There are so many things to consider when purchasing a drone. Matching the right camera to the right drone is also a hassle. Since this is just the beginning of this emerging market, the options are really fragmented, and I have found it very difficult to choose. Nevertheless, we get one shot at getting it right, so I spent the better part of a few days calling camera shops and drone shops, visiting with the local rc store, calling random companies who are advertising drone services in other parts of the United States and watching YouTube videos that compare drones and cameras. Since I cannot afford the DJI S1000 copter, I have decided to go with another Phantom with a H3-3D gymbal and Go Pro Hero 3+ Black Edition. This set up is something we can afford and gives us flexibility to get extra blades and batteries and to buy insurance. Our hope is that the quality is high enough that developers find it acceptable.[41] We can then save our money to be able to buy the higher quality S1000 as well as a Panasonic GH4 camera.

Park Ave/Project XiP

In the last week the Park Ave team spent a lot of time contacting businesses and homeowners in the Norman area to see if they would sign up for Park Ave's service in preparation of OU football season. Sadly, the team was not able to get any home or business to sign up. So we redirected our attention to the University's sale of parking on game days. Today, we met with the director of OU's Parking and Transportation services and, again, we were told that Park Ave did not add enough value to them as a seller in order to be used.

So the Park Ave team has decided to transition to a project already begun by team member, Shelby Vanhooser. The new technology will be able to track the flow of cars in and out of various parking lots and provide useful data to both parkers and lot owners. OU Parking and Transportation has already expressed interest in using the application.

---

41 My feedback was that they don't need to "hope"! It is possible to test the quality of the photos and whether they are acceptable to the target market before buying the equipment. A good test is to download several types of example photos, at different sizes and resolutions, and then show them to potential clients for feedback.

ACCELERATOR WEEK 4—TEAM BLOG POSTS

The team decided to see if other universities would be interested in a similar technology, and we emailed 17 different directors of parking services at universities in Oklahoma and Texas. Almost immediately we had responses to set up phone meetings—5 in total in less than two hours! We are so excited to see where this new venture will take us.

The XiP team will be conducting two experiments this week. One will be to test technology and the other to test the business side of XiP. The team's first hypothesis is that we can install XiP's current technology on a parking lot entrance/exit at a lot at OU and get a 95 percent accuracy rate at counting cars. To test this, the XiP team will install the technology and then hand count cars in the parking lot and cross compare those numbers to the numbers counted by XiP. If we do not get a 95 percent success rate, then the XiP team will begin to explore different technologies to get that 95 percent accuracy rate.

The next hypothesis XiP will test is that after pitching our product to a university within driving distance of OU, they will be willing to have us come and install XiP on one of their parking lots. To test this, the team will continue to follow up and have meetings with different directors of parking services at universities in Oklahoma and ask them if they would be willing to have us come install one. If no one allows us to come out, then we will need to rethink our pitch/value prop so that schools will be willing to have XiP installed.

CLASS 9, WEEK 5—CUSTOMER RELATIONSHIPS

Picking up some initial traction

Half way through the Accelerator we started seeing some progress. Driven Analytics made their first sales to car dealerships to run a pilot of their program with ten cars. Levaté had a website[42] up, a video of a prototype,[43] and had started a funding conversation with i2e. Park Ave made a big decision to pivot away from connecting buyers and sellers of parking spaces at big events in Norman after running a variety of experiments that did not turn up any customers. They decided to start working on a device that could count cars going in and out of parking lots to help universities keep track of their parking spot usage rates. And within a few hours of making the pivot, they already had excited university parking directors returning their cold calls!

Once a young company starts getting traction from potential customers, the feedback loop becomes much stronger and the company can focus on their niche, rather than spinning around trying to find a customer at all. They can also then start getting into other interesting questions beyond, "Does anyone even want this?"

Staying the course

During the updates and news section that I started the first class of the week with, I urged and cautioned the teams to stick with the

---

42 levatelift.com
43 https://www.youtube.com/watch?v=xr8B6mkWaUw#t=27

program. Running experiments and testing before building is the name of the game and must continue even after a few customers start nibbling on the hook. It was an exciting moment for sure but not a reason to abandon the game plan. I also told the teams their blogs were extremely helpful to me and to continue writing them and including as much detail about the experiments as possible.

Finally, I asked for a 60-minute one-on-one meeting with each team. One of my hypotheses from before the summer started was that the teams would take advantage of open office hours to discuss their experiments and progress with me. That hypothesis was invalidated, as I only had a handful of office hours. My guess was that the teams get enough of my feedback during our two scheduled class sessions and dinner each week and use their remaining time out in the field and working on their product. I used this meeting to review the team's business model canvas, recap the experiments they've run, make a plan for the final month, and give more targeted feedback than I do in class.

Customer Relationships

Steve Blank defines customer relationships as the interplay of customers, sales channel, value prop, and marketing. It's the more holistic side of thinking about your customer and is highly relevant to the teams. Selling a wheelchair lift to an end user who expects it to simply work for 5–10 years after the purchase is a very different type of relationship than one in which a drone team that wants to engage with a construction company every week for the life of a large building project.

Another way to think about customer relationships is to consider everything that happens *after* the initial sale. Steve Blank provides a nifty chart for that, which I've borrowed from the Lean Launchpad.[44]

---

[44] http://steveblank.com/category/lean-launchpad/

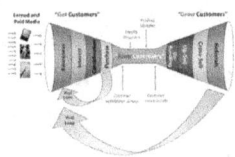

Get, Keep, Grow

This is a generic customer life-cycle journey

Get—first a company finds potential customers and adds them to the top (or side, in this case) of the funnel. Then the customer learns about the company and the product and eventually buys or uses the product.

Keep—This is basically customer service! The startup wants to provide the best possible experience for each customer.

Grow—This phase includes two key components: (1) providing additional value to the customer so the customer purchases more from the company, and (2) the customer 's enjoying the product so much she refers the company to other customers. Point no. 2 is also called a viral loop and allows a startup to achieve high growth.

One key point about scaling after finding traction is that one passed test does *not* create a business. The hypothesis-experiment-results model is still the best way to scale a business. The thought should be, validate, scale and repeat!

Another important idea is that any cost the company incurs getting a customer to purchase is part of the cost-to-acquire (CTA), and the value of the customer from purchase through referral is the customer's lifetime value (LTV). At the heart of a business model is whether the CTA is less than the LTV. If yes, the company can make a profit off of each customer. If no, the company is going to go out of business unless it makes a change.

I once again had drawing the sales cycle and customer persona on the agenda, but the teams didn't think that would be a good use of class time. Since the start of the summer, we had decided to shrink class time down to two hours from three, to leave more time for outside-the-class activities, especially during key working hours. That put pressure on some of the activities and exercises I wanted to do.

CLASS 9, WEEK 5—CUSTOMER RELATIONSHIPS

I still think drawing is a good way of making sure a team has a grasp on these two ideas. One line I really like from the Lean Launchpad in regards to building customer personas is, "Do you know what your customers read, what trade shows they attend, what gurus they follow, and where they turn for new product information?" The better you know and understand your customer, the more likely you are to build something they want to use or buy.

CLASS 10, WEEK 5—DIGITAL MARKETING (PAID ADS FOCUS)

Just past the halfway mark for the ten-week Accelerator, the teams asked if we could look at how paid advertising works, particularly for Google and Facebook. This is a class I teach all the time and that I wrote a book on,[45] and it is how I first got started teaching about marketing and entrepreneurship. In many ways it feels like coming home each time I teach this class!

I follow this worksheet when teaching digital marketing: Digital Marketing for Business Growth.[46] Because that worksheet was coupled with an all-day class and we only had 2 hours, I decided to focus in on the foundations of digital marketing and then jump to paid ads.

Demographics

Digital marketing always starts with the demographic the company wants to target. The teams already have done a lot of work defining their customer (in Lean Startup/Launchpad, this is called the customer persona), so this kickoff wasn't too difficult.

Digital channels

There are three main digital channels that startups should be concerned with. These are also called owned media, because the startup has

---

45 http://amzn.to/UXT2aL
46 http://ericmorrow.com/wp-content/uploads/Digital-Marketing-for-Business-Growth-with-TOC.pdf

CLASS 10. WEEK 5—DIGITAL MARKETING (PAID ADS FOCUS)

control over them. They are website, social media, and email. We went through the exercise of thinking about the type of content that goes into each channel and the main take-away for each: website—answer common customer questions; social—zoom out from your business; and email—every email to your customer database needs to be a gift.

I have two full classes on paid advertising available on YouTube for free.

Class 1—http://www.youtube.com/watch?v=79k2b34CcMQ

Class 2—http://www.youtube.com/watch?v=2kB7NLc4QZY

Target preaggregated groups

In short, a startup can buy ads in order to put their messaging in front of an audience that has been aggregated by someone else. For example, Google aggregates people who are searching for certain things by the keywords they type into the Google search box, and then sells ads to the search results. Facebook aggregates people interested in sharing photos and status updates and shows ads that are based on their expressed interests. And blogs aggregate people who are interested in the same topic—for example, exercise or cooking—and sells ads that are based on those interests.

Regardless of the platform, the first step in running an ad is to decide *who the ad is going to target*—ie: the demographic! It could be based on, for example, keywords searches, demographics, or expressed interests.

The second step is to decide on the *content of the ad*. Different platforms have different requirements (ie: Google is normally all text, Facebook has a small picture). The common denominator is usually to make a compelling offer. For example, "Sign up to be a beta tester for a new wheelchair lift," or "Take weekly photos of your construction site."

The third step is to take the person who clicks on your ad to a *well-constructed landing page*. Check out unbounce.com for my favorite resource on landing pages. In general, the landing page should be a continuation of the offer and should ask the visitor to do something.

CLASS 10, WEEK 5—DIGITAL MARKETING (PAID ADS FOCUS)

Usual actions are to buy something or leave their email to get more information.

That was about as much of a crash course in digital marketing and paid advertising as I could fit into 2 hours. We also touched briefly on maintaining a good email database with all of the company's customers and interested leads. Finally, we took a quick look at how Google analytics, tied with Goals, can tell you how effective your website is.

We may return to digital marketing if the teams need help with finding more leads and moving leads through the sales process.

ACCELERATOR WEEK 5—TEAM BLOG POSTS

Levaté

FACEBOOK ADS AND DELAYED CYLINDERS

It's been a whirlwind week! We've been on the phone with customer service reps trying to locate lost pneumatic cylinders, learning the basics of digital marketing and online ads, and also making plenty of phone calls trying to understand more about the insurance reimbursement process for wheelchair accessories.

LEVATÉ IS MOBILE

There is some good news to report on the prototyping! Take a look at the pictures below of Ethan operating the lift with 125 lbs of weight on top. It's using small pneumatic cylinders of 0.5 inch diameter that can support less weight but are cheap and quick to prototype with. Also, notice that the lift is connected to an air tank—a paintball air tank actually—so the lift is mobile as well!

ACCELERATOR WEEK 5—TEAM BLOG POSTS

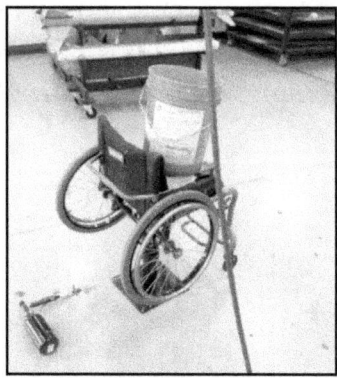

The .5 inch bore cylinders lifting 125lbs. of weight, powered by a paintball air tank compressed to 3000psi.

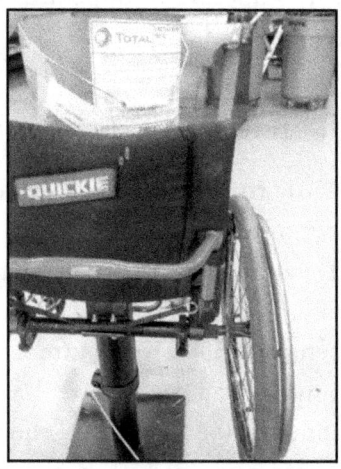

Today and tomorrow we'll be working on using the new, thicker cylinders we just bought to build a prototype that can lift our full 300 lb. goal.

That part of the prototyping was a bit delayed, unfortunately. We overnight ordered two 2.5-inch bore, 6-inch stroke pneumatic cylinders. They should have arrived last Thursday morning. The package finally came in on Friday, but with only 1 cylinder! A call to customer service confirmed that a mistake had been made in their shipping, and we received the second cylinder on Saturday. It set our prototyping back a few days, though I will say that Sherry, the woman we spoke to at the Industrial Supply store who was managing our order, was incredibly helpful and apologetic throughout the entire process.

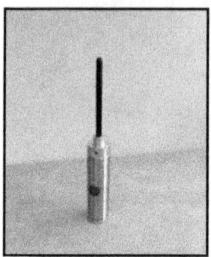

One of two cylinders which we'll be attaching together in "piggyback" orientation, to operate in opposite directions and thus get double the lift of a single cylinder.

FACEBOOK ADVERTISEMENTS

Last week, we signed up to run a series of four Facebook ads to understand (1) what sort of engagement and response could we expect from such ads; and (2) what content in the Facebook ads would be most effective. After four days of ads, a reach of 17,000 Facebook users, and $70 total spent, we have some interesting results.

For the sake of simplicity, let's say we had 2 ads, with written messages (limited to about 150 characters), code-named ads 1 & 2.

When a Facebook user saw ad 1, they either saw picture A or B, but not both. Ad 2, on the other hand, demonstrated either picture B or picture C to users. This way, we could tell not only which ad text message was more effective by comparing the engagement results across picture B but also which pictures were more effective, by comparing specifically those within the Ad 1 and Ad 2 messages.

Here are the results:
1. Ad message 1 with picture A had 39 website clicks and 10 post likes, with a click-through rate of 3.3%. The click-through rate is how many people out of a hundred actually clicked on the ad. It reached 1400 people.

2. Ad message 1 with picture B had 10 likes, 2 shares, and 24 clicks, and had a click-through rate of 2.3%. It reached about 2000 people.
3. Ad message 2 with picture B had 21 clicks, 7 likes, and 2 shares, with a click-through rate of 0.8%. It reached 2300 people.
4. Ad message 2 with picture C had 198 clicks, 23 likes, and 8 shares, but only had a click-through rate of 1% because of its very high reach (12,000).

These results indicate that ad message 1 is clearly superior to 2, and that picture A is superior to B & C. Here was the winning ad:

Levaté is a 12 inch lift for manual chairs for extra reach at home, the office, or a store

INSURANCE INDUSTRY HASSLES

That just leaves the last of our tests this week to talk about, The Insurance Question, or: Can Levaté be insurance reimbursable?

We had heard anecdotal evidence that power lift devices might be considered medically necessary by insurance if they were instrumental in helping the user transfer in and out of their power chair, for example. Our thoughts are that we could make a similar argument for Levaté, and we wanted to talk to a decision maker in the industry to confirm this and understand what process a wheelchair user would need to go through to get a Levaté unit reimbursed by their insurance company.

First, the good news! It looks like the process for registering a product with the Department of Veteran's Affairs (VA) is very straightforward: you go to sam.gov and complete a registration process there for the device. Once it's registered, the VA will pay for 100% of the device. The only hard part after that is generating the word-of-mouth among wheelchair users and physical therapists (PTs): The former so that they ask their PTs for them, and the latter so that they recommend Levaté to their patients. If a purchase is under $3,000, then it's approved immediately by the local VA hospital with a minimum of red tape.

On the other hand, it looks like both manufacturers and wheelchair users are opting out of medical reimbursement entirely.

One wheelchair accessory manufacturer explained why they opted out of trying to get their device (the FreeWheel[47]) coded by insurance companies. The fee you pay Medicare—who sets the trends for the entire industry—is $50,000 just to begin the coding process. And there's no guarantee that the insurance code will be approved. Even if it is, you pay $8,000 annually to maintain the code, and insurance providers can still deny a claim for that code if they feel there's a reason to (ie, if they can save money and get away with it).

Wheelchair users are also opting out of insurance due to the hassle and 6–12 month wait. That means that a wheelchair user with a chair that's falling apart could wait up to a year from the time they file their insurance paperwork before they get their new chair, as was the case for one of the wheelchair users we spoke with a couple days ago.

Scott at Tri State Medical, a wheelchair dealer, noted that 30–40% of his customers opt out of trying to get insurance to reimburse their purchases and instead pay for their new wheelchairs out of pocket. This is even moreso the case for purchases under $1,000. At $500, he said most wheelchair users won't even bother trying to get a device reimbursed by their insurance—it's just not worth it.

Clearly there are some things very wrong with the American insurance system. Until there is industry-wide reform, we can at least

---

[47] http://www.gofreewheel.gov/

equip wheelchair users with the tools they need to try for insurance reimbursement of Levaté with their private insurance. Freewheel, which I mentioned above, provides instructions for wheelchair users[48] on their website to get their doctors or PTs to prescribe their accessory in such a way that it is seen as a medical necessity and can be covered under the "Miscellaneous Wheelchair Accessory" code K0108. This may be the best work-around for those who have private insurance and can't afford Levaté on their own.

That's what the Levaté team has been up to this past week. If you have any experience with the insurance industry or reimbursement process and would like to comment on the process or what we've found so far, we'd love to hear from you! You can comment here, send an email to levatelift@gmail.com or find us on Facebook[49] and Twitter.[50]

Driven Analytics

Hardware has finally arrived! We received 30 dongles on Monday afternoon and are expecting to receive the SIM cards any day. There is no doubt a lot of configuration work that will have to be done to get these things ready to deploy to customers, but we are at least on the right track.

Although it only took a week for devices to arrive after the PO and payment was processed, it did take about a week just to get to the point of processing the PO. There were a number of technical interchanges and questions that went back and forth, and the quality of customer service has been variegated, good at times and poor at others. This is something we will have to monitor as we go forward.

This week, there will be two experiments to conduct related to the SLP accelerator. In addition, there is a heavy focus on wrapping up legal matters with the formation of Driven Analytics, as well as handling all of the new hardware, etc.

---

48 https://www.gofreewheel.com/fw/FreeWheel-and-Insurance
49 http://facebook.com/levatelift
50 http://twitter.com/levatelift

Experiment 1:

Hypothesis: Floor plan companies are interested in using our technology to lower their risk and save time by tracking assets.

Test: Send marketing materials and see if we can get an in-person meeting to further discuss.

Results: I went back and forth with my contact to hone in on the price point and some other factors that would be important but wasn't able to get much further. In the end, I sent a one page marketing brochure that was selling a "beta" test with Driven Analytics. I don't think I'm going to get any takers because the price is just so high right now that I can't offer them a good value.

Insights: Get more information about the real pain of these companies and hone the pitch. Perhaps the value with these guys is getting them to offer a price break for dealerships using our system, which would increase value for the dealerships.

Experiment 2:

Hypothesis: Much could be learned by shadowing a service writer at one or both of our test dealerships, and the dealerships would be open to allow this to happen.

Test: Ask both dealerships if I can do about a half day of shadowing in order to understand their biggest customer challenges, etc.

Results: This test got nowhere. Both dealerships were unresponsive and just had too much going on with end of month and 4th of July weekend sales. This is still a valuable test, and I will rerun it again.

Insights: The engagement of dealerships is probably going to be harder than I thought, even after they have paid. I am probably going to have to find a way to set up shop or make my presence there regular in order to have any chance at establishing a real relationship with them that is mutually beneficial.

Other matters that took a huge part of my week last week were regarding personnel and legal issues. I spent over 30 hours working on matters related to formation, equity and service agreements etc., and this week more time will be spent on that stuff. This is disappointing, as these things are massively distracting from the more important matters: customer and technology development.

We are scheduled to have our final formation meeting, which will include signing all of the documents and issuing stock certificates on Wednesday night! Finally...we will be official and we can move on.

Sowers Publishing

Week 5 Experiments

1. Someone will pay $150 for a quality Bible with note pages.
2. We can get a booth to sell Bibles at this summer.
3. We can get a summer camp to commit to using our services for next summer.

Icarus Aerial Technologies

Piggybacking off of last week's need to try more construction companies, we called 30 more construction companies this week. Our goal was 50, but we did not reach that number. Calling these companies took much longer than anticipated. Some phone calls ended up taking 30 minutes to close to an hour by the time you look up the company, find the number or appropriate person to call, write their information into the CRM, and call them. Many of the conversations lasted 30 or more minutes themselves. I was expecting to be able to call a company every 5 minutes or so, but that was not close to enough time to be able to actually complete a phone call.

Some of the issue was a good thing. The construction companies I called were interested and helpful. They gave me unsolicited advice and other help. It was the first sign of a consumer base that was genuinely interested in what we had to offer. Out of the 30 construction companies that we contacted, 5 were interested enough to agree to have us come out and shoot a construction site for free. Some of the issue I had was getting past the gatekeeper. When I actually was able to speak with one of the owners or someone in charge, I got a good result. When the gatekeeper took a message for me or had me leave a voice mail message, I didn't get results. With construction companies, the people who make decisions spend the majority of their time in the field and not at their desk. Getting in touch with those people is a tough task. These are large companies, and I can tell that the secretary is often hesitant to allow me to speak with someone live. I would say that our result was encouraging. We definitely found more interest with construction companies than with farmers and real estate agents. This would be our third pivot, and it seems that we might have found a viable product market fit. More testing needs to be done this week.

Some of the holdup is our product. We have still not received the check cards from the small business account that we opened. This, in turn, means that we have not been able to order the appropriate drone. As a result, we have to simply tell the interested parties that we will be out to photograph their construction yard as soon as our gear arrives. I have been back and forth with the bank in fixing this issue, and I hope to have it resolved today. It is crucial that we get our drone ordered in the next day or two so we can move forward with testing.

Park Ave/Project XiP

This week the XiP team continued to talk to the parking directors of universities in the Southwest. Our business hypothesis this week was that if we pitched our idea to university parking directors, they would be willing to have us come out to beta test our product with them. The test was to continue our meetings with parking directors, discuss their current pain points and then close the conversation with a pitch and the big question, "when we have a technology ready to test, can we come to your university and beta test on one of your parking lots?"

We had seven meetings with directors and have gotten six to agree to beta. Through this experiment we gained insights about what directors want (reliable and cost-effective technologies) and about the size of universities that would like a technology like ours (20,000–30,000 student, faculty and staff body).

On the tech side we wanted to test the accuracy of our current technology. Currently, our technology uses inductor loops to track the flow of cars. We had a hypothesis that we could get this technology to count cars in and out of a parking lot at OU with a 95 percent accuracy rate. To test this, we were going to use XiP on a parking lot and then count the cars in the parking lot through the day and compare the numbers. Unfortunately, one of the exits on the parking lot went bad and the university's hardware went crazy and couldn't track exiting cars. Since this hypothesis was invalidated, we are going to move to image processing–based technologies.

CLASS 11, WEEK 6—REVENUE STREAMS

After 6 weeks, I wanted to meet with each team one on one to get a deeper progress report, check on the current status of the business model canvas assumptions (meaning, can the company make money as it is currently positioned?), and set in place a good plan for the sprint to the finish line. Rehearsal day is a short 3 weeks away!

I started class by asking for questions about accounting and finance, because Pat Jones, CFO from Petra Industries[51] (and formerly Hobby Lobby), is coming in to teach. Here are the questions that were posed:

- How to keep books balanced and legal

- Rundown of balance sheet, income statement, statement of cash flows, and how they correlate

- Taxes—How to file taxes and how to approach personal taxes on the $10,000 investment they got from OU (most are LLCs)

- Double-entry accounting intro

- Essential guidelines on business expenses and taxes

- How to maximize a small amount of cash, leverage investors

- W2 and 1099 employees—withholding and filing quarterly (escrow accounts?)

I had originally envisioned the teams teaching more of the classes themselves, since I believe there is no better way to learn a subject

---

51 http://www.petra.com/

than to teach it. Ultimately, I scrapped that idea. I preferred to keep the teams laser focused on their customer and product development. However, the day before the rehearsal dinner I asked the students to meet and help each other prepare. During our last pitch session I felt the teams gave each other great advice, so I'm confident they will once again do so. I would like to experiment in the future with removing myself from the equation and forcing the teams to rely more on each other for feedback.

Update on experiments

As always, the teams started the day by presenting the results of their last week's experiments. They followed the formula of hypothesis, test, results, and insights. I thought after 6 weeks of going through this process it would have become second nature, but the teams have varying levels of comfort with presenting their ideas in this manner. I need to think more about how I teach the students to present their ideas and come up with new exercises to improve this ability. I rely very heavily on practice and real-time feedback, and it seems more is needed. I think next time I would have the teams present their results in writing first, in advance of class, so I could review it earlier. And then work one on one with teams that were having trouble.

We then discussed the next box in the business model canvas—Revenue Streams. Steve Blank defines "Revenue Model" as the strategy the company uses to generate cash from each customer segment. In short, it's how the company gets paid. When devising the revenue strategy, each customer segment needs its own revenue model.

A key question that always comes up for new companies is how to price their product. The specific dollars and cents that make up pricing is called a tactic and is different from a revenue model, which is more of a strategy for converting customer value into money. In addition, revenue streams are not income statements, balance sheets, and cash flow. Those are accounting terms, and while critical for the startup's health, do not describe how the company makes money.

Blank identifies a variety of types of revenue streams.

CLASS 11, WEEK 6—REVENUE STREAMS

- Asset sale—like an apple or a house (you buy it, you own it)

- Usage fee—like Amazon web services or electricity (the more you use, the more you pay)

- Subscription—like a newspaper or SaaS (repeating fee over a set period)

- Renting—like hardware or houses (use it as much as you like during a set period)

- Licensing—like IP (you can use the IP, but you don't own it)

- Intermediation—like eBay or Airbnb (connect two sides of a market, take a transaction fee)

- Advertising—like magazines or Google (sell ads next to the primary content)

A good jumping off point for thinking about revenue streams is to ask how customers are paying for your type of product today. In some cases, you'll want to follow the same model, since that's what consumers are already familiar with. But disruption frequently occurs when you find a different revenue model. Zipcar started by renting cars by the hour, not by the day, like most car rental companies. Google charged advertisers by the click, not by the number of viewers. Amazon web services charge by usage, rather than selling the underlying hardware.

Another big question is whether you price your product on cost or value. I think it's always a good idea to go for value! Don't start with how much the product costs to make. Think from the customer's perspective and find out how much they are willing to pay for the value you bring them. This is a common pitfall for new companies, who often set prices on the basis of a markup over their costs.

The teams then presented their current thinking on revenue streams for their business, and we closed with the presentation of new experiments for the week, which you'll again see in the weekly team updates.

CLASS 12, WEEK 6—STORYBOARDING

For this week's Startup Skills class, we did one of my absolute favorites: storyboarding! Anytime you've seen an intro or explanatory video on the web, it started as a storyboard.

Introducing explanatory videos

I began the class with a few videos to get everyone's creative juices going. (Note: if you want to see all these videos in one place without typing in the respective URLs, go to this page on my blog.[52])

Kickoff videos

Coin[53] (my personal favorite). This video has it all. Good storytelling, clear product vision, nice production values, and good pace.

Groupon[54] (30 seconds!). This video is a great introduction to the product, is very short and animated.

Who Gives A Crap?[55] Nothing holds people's attention like humor. This video has a crap-ton of that.

Colspace[56] (disclaimer: I created this one). I like to show the Colspace video because it shows what is good enough to get the point across. The video cost less than $3,000 to make and quickly and

---

52 http://ericmorrow.com/2014/07/02/class-12-week-6-storyboarding/
53 https://www.youtube.com/watch?v=w9Sx34swEG0
54 http://vimeo.com/12825301
55 https://www.youtube.com/watch?v=WdWZ8WVv6qk
56 https://www.youtube.com/watch?v=aewjFS_DVDU

CLASS 12, WEEK 6—STORYBOARDING

clearly conveys what Colspace does (so long as you are in the intended demographic).

After each one, I asked the students to say what they liked and disliked about each video. This gave the class an interesting baseline to start from.

First round storyboard

I then asked the students to come up with their own explanatory video storyboard. Each student worked alone to increase the number of initial ideas we created. After 5 minutes of sketching and brainstorming, the students shared their ideas with each other through a short acting out of the video idea. Acting out was a recommendation from Mathilde Verdier at UNC's the Cube for Social Entrepreneurship[57] and has turned out to be very popular!

Get excited!!

And then I showed them Solar Freaking' Roadways. I started with the Indiegogo page.[58]

Consider the first video

Solar Roadways produced.[59] Sadly, it is quite boring. The presentation is monotone, the production quality is low, and it takes forever to get to the point. But then consider the second video.[60] It is exactly the opposite: high energy and attention-grabbing.

This is the launching off point for a different style from what most people come up with at first, which tends to be straightforward and relatively low energy. Launching new products can be fun and interesting as well as helpful!

So the students went back to the drawing board and come up with a totally different version of their storyboard, this time with high-

---

57 http://campus-y.unc.edu/incubator
58 https://www.indiegogo.com/projects/solar-roadways
59 https://www.youtube.com/watch?v=SNMFKKyFU60
60 https://www.youtube.com/watch?v=qlTA3rnpgzU

energy, in your face action! I also asked them to start thinking about patterns and repetition. You only need to get one or two ideas across in a 60-second video, and those ideas should be repeated a handful of times for maximum stickiness. At the end of the second iteration, the students once again shared their storyboards with the group by acting them out.

Round three: Something you'll actually use
I started off round three by again showing a few videos to get the ideas moving and asking the students what they like and dislike.

Pepple[61]
Zencash[62] (drawing)
Dropbox[63]
The Girl Effect[64]

The goal of the class was to have the teams walk away with a storyboard they could actually make into a video. For example, here's a video put together by Kevin Hicks for Triangle Bikeworks[65] after a storyboarding class at the Cube at UNC.

The goal isn't to be perfect! It's to get a first draft of the video out to your customers so you can get feedback.

So here, for your viewing pleasure, are what the teams came up with! The link is to a YouTube channel

with many videos from the summer—look for the ones that say Storyboard Presentation.[66]

---

61 https://www.kickstarter.com/projects/597507018/pebble-e-paper-watch-for-iphone-and-android
62 https://www.youtube.com/watch?v=VxgDuqmlEQk
63 https://www.youtube.com/watch?v=w4eTR7tci6A
64 https://www.youtube.com/watch?v=1e8xgF0JtVg
65 https://www.youtube.com/watch?v=R-4BJwjU57Q
66 https://www.youtube.com/playlist?list=PLPg5JK84K1AjIQF-XYck_eoivO0BmVdsv

ACCELERATOR WEEK 6—TEAM BLOG POSTS

Levaté

TESTS FOR NEXT WEEK: SOCIAL MEDIA, VA, AND PROTOTYPING

What's up everyone! I hope you're all enjoying the World Cup USA–Germany match right now.

Quick update on what the team's working on over the next week.
1. Can we get just as much user activity from social media content as we did with our Facebook ads in 1 week's time? That means getting about 10 beta test users and 10 newsletter subscribers to sign up on this website.
2. Can we get our wheelchair lift into the VA hospital computer system and have a veteran request one of their occupational therapists or PTs? This is to understand the process for when we are manufacturing the final version of the wheelchair lift and are trying to get it in the hands of wheelchair users.
3. Can we have a wheelchair user test a working prototype, and get feedback from them on it? Obviously, this will be huge for us.

Those are our tests for this week. Go USA—We believe that we will win!

Driven Analytics

The weeks are flying by! It is hard to believe that the Accelerator will be over in just a few more weeks.

Although we are transitioning in the Accelerator to the pitch day, we will continue to run experiments in our quest to reach a level of validation that will inspire a VC investment.

In this week's experiments, I will repeat one of last week's experiments and do one new one.

Experiment 1:

Hypothesis: Much could be learned by shadowing a service writer at one or both of our test dealerships. and the dealerships would be open to allow this to happen.

Test: Ask both dealerships if I can do about a half day of shadowing in order to understand their biggest customer challenges, etc.

Results: Success! On Friday I was able to spend time with the service manager, including listening in on about a 30-minute conversation with the Nissan warranty and service rep, where he must have said the phrase "customer retention" about 10 times. Nissan is putting a huge emphasis on better and faster service by having a new "express" service, where a customer should be able to be in and out of the dealership in 30 minutes. After spending time with the service manager, I shadowed the express service writer for the rest of the afternoon. I observed 16 cars come into service, and none of them made it out in less than an hour. I plan to go back and shadow a service advisor (the ones that do more complex services) next week. I also have an appointment scheduled to shadow in the service department at a different Nissan for this Wednesday.

Insights: Dealerships have a LONG way to go in the service world. The express service writers were basically taking orders, not thoughtfully reviewing a customer's vehicle and suggesting services. In the one case where a fuel injector cleaning was suggested, the lady asked why and the service writer couldn't give her a good answer. She declined the service but still spent over 2 hours waiting on her vehicle.

ACCELERATOR WEEK 6—TEAM BLOG POSTS

Experiment 2:

Hypothesis: If we ask our mobile device supplier for the SDK, they will give it to us for free.

Test: Ask Jonna for the SDK in an email. If she resists, set up a meeting where we can give them information about our business plan and what we will be doing.

Results: Fail...the problems we had getting our initial devices launched this week caused us to turn all of our focus with our supplier towards support of our current products rather than working on any new arrangements. We will pursue this once we have the 20 devices we tried to get up and running installed and on their way.

Other things this week included finally getting the company formed. We met downtown on Wednesday and got the documents signed, and besides a few loose ends to tie up, we are pretty much done with formation.

Also, we scored a meeting with all of the GMs from a large group of dealers last week, and it was very positive. We met with them on Wednesday, and all the GMs were very interested in what we were doing. The manager for the Chevy store did have some concern with interference happening between our devices and some of the electronics on GM vehicles, as they have had some issues come up with people using the insurance OBD2 devices. I will spend some time at that dealership doing testing on various vehicles to see if we will have similar issues.

Hours for this week were moving in the right direction, with more time spent on customer development and less time on administrative stuff.

Administrative: 13:15
Customer Development: 17:45
SLP activities: 9
Total: 40

Sowers Publishing

Step 1. Ask someone what their perfect Bible would be.
Step 2. Build it.
Step 3. Give it to them (or better yet, ask them to pay for it).
Step 4. See if they use it.
Because of what I learned at Mardel, I will now focus on...

Meeting with Mardel (Thursday)

On Thursday morning, Pat Jones and I met with Dee Ann Anderson, director of merchandising at Mardel. Dee Ann chooses all products that are sold in Mardel and has a team of buyers who travel the country looking for new and exciting products, often having changes made so that Mardel can sell them. Pat was able to set this up because he was the CFO for Hobby Lobby for many years.

Sitting down with Dee Ann, it was apparent that Pat had not told her much more than that I was a student looking to have some questions answered. She admitted to being caught off guard after I gave the explanation of who I was and what I was trying to do. However, she was pleasantly surprised and began to give me everything she could think of on the subject. She told us that she has dreams of one day doing that out of the back of Mardel's stores instead of stocking inventory, simply print on demand. The setback for Mardel hit me like a sack of bricks; they struggle to attain copyright privileges as well. This was the biggest challenge I have faced so far, and the place I go in hopes of answers tells me they are struggling with the same problem. Additionally, when they want books/Bibles printed, they get put on a waiting list because the printers have such a large demand. This makes no sense to me because Hobby Lobby could easily afford to buy Mardel the printing equipment and warehouse space to do their own printing. They also helped to create the Digital Bible Library and should have access to it as easy as anyone. I believe the other publishing companies that own the copyrights to the popular versions do not want Mardel to gain access to them because they would turn around, print their own Bibles, and challenge the business of current sellers. After hearing Dee Ann, the system is "working," and they are looking for "traditional" and nearly riskless areas for sales growth.

One of the most important things I was able to get from this meeting was that Dee Ann, who has been asking customers what they want and successfully buying products to match their needs since the '70s refused to help me validate that customers would pay top dollar for a custom Bible. She said that after speaking with thousands of customers, she would put the future of Mardel on the line that people will pay for this product if it was offered today. She begged me not to spend another dime reaching out to find validation for that and promised I would be wasting my money. In fact, the only time she turned down something I asked of her was for that. I spent the rest of the day trying to wrap my mind around the sternness she had on that subject. Was it because they had tried before and failed? Maybe because over the years she has lost count of the times people asked her for a custom Bible. It could also be that Mardel is in the middle of doing that and she doesn't want me to get in the way of her success. Doubtful, but I have to put it out there. Whatever it was, I feel torn to find my own validation, taking a chance of wasting my time and money, or to trust the advice of someone in a position to help me and spend my time and money moving forward to new validations beyond customers. We'll see what happens after a weekend of prayer.

Things I asked Dee Ann's help with:
1. If Mardel does their own printing, are they willing to partner to print together?
   a. "We do not do print the Bible. We do small printing, but nothing close to the level you would need." However, someone who worked for her for over 20 years was recently given an executive position at LOOP Publishing, the world's largest Bible publishing company. She offered to put me in contact with him and see if he can help with either copyright permissions or the printing of the physical Bibles.
2. Can you help me gain access to the Digital Bible Library?

    a. "That is outside my expertise. I know that will not be easy, but if there's anyone in the world who can you, it's Mart. He would love your vision, and you couldn't get him to tell you about his vision unless you have some serious free time. I think you will really benefit from that. Let me see if I can get you in with him." **(The following day Mart's secretary emailed me and scheduled a meeting for July 25th!!)**
3. Can I send out to Mardel's customer email list with a link to a survey?
    a. "hahaha no." Then she gave me the explanation that I was wasting my time if I continued to seek customer validation. I knew that was out of the question, but I couldn't let her leave the room thinking that she gave me access to everything they had available. #PowerNegotiating

Survey Monkey (Friday)

Survey Monkey is a great way for us to buy leads. They have the ability for us to create a survey asking any questions we would like. For a minimum of $1,500 they will provide a team manager for us to help develop the most attractive survey. Additionally, with a team manager we are able to specifically target Christians or nominations of Christianity. We can exclude certain demographics as well. Moreover, with this team we are able to receive basic geographic and demographic information, without including those types of questions in our survey. This helps because the shorter the survey is, the more attention participants will have throughout the survey, hopefully leading to more in-depth and truthful information. Because some of our questions will have a textbox for a written answer, we will need to be able to pull out keywords and phrases. Right now, we are paying $26 per month for basic Survey Monkey membership that allows us unlimited surveys, 1,000 responses per month and other small features. Our team manager offered us a free Gold membership upgrade for a year (worth $300) included in the $1,500. This is valuable because this upgrade will give us text analytics, as well the ability to automatically redirect participants to any website after the completion of our survey. This will allow us to take people directly to our website or landing page at the completion of our survey. The best part of this service is the ability to ask questions in our survey that if answered in a specific way, their survey will be discarded from the results and will not count as a survey submission, helping to avoid costly surveys that will give us information we do not need. Each survey costs $3.25, reaching 462 people who specifically fit our target market for only $1,501.50. The cost of a lead at $3.25 is relatively cheap, especially for how direct the marketing channel is. If we want to reach more people, they have a few thousand people that fit our specific target.

Elance (Friday & Monday)

People on Elance are horrible to work with! Everyone types in broken English and uses terminology I do not understand. Before a job is awarded, everyone says, "No problem. Easy work. A few hours tops. Hire me so I can start." And then once awarded a job, they go to, "I want you to skype me. Did you say X? Because it seems like you said X, but I want to make sure it's not X & Y. Hey, how much you pay if I do X & Y? Please download program so you can download and see the work I did for you. I know I was a pain in the butt, but I would love to work with you again." And the best and most common: "Give me 5 stars!" Though not a single one of them so far has done 5-star work! Needless to say, I am struggling to get the work I need done on there. They need my help constantly, but they are only working from our midnight to 2:00 pm and then get frustrated if I happen to not email them back immediately.

All that aside, we now have a digital file of the entire New Testament and will soon have the entire Old Testament. This was done in American Standard Version (ASV) so that we can avoid copyright laws and sell anything we print. We had them put together from individual rtf book folders to both .docx and .pdf in folders sorted by book, including individual pages saved separately. This has cost less than $200 so far, which is more than I wanted to pay on Elance, but way less than I expected overall.

I would like to do the same thing with the King James Version (KJV) soon. This might allow us to give people we are currently building Bibles for an option for something more traditional.

I have found that Elance can be useful for other jobs as well. I am currently bidding out a checklist that can be turned into a heat map for experiment 3. I am beginning to meet more dedicated and professional people as well.

Week 6 Experiments (2 WEEK EXPERIMENTS)

1. **We can form a strategic partnership with Mardel to attain copyright privileges and/or the means necessary to print.**

Why? Because we must have copyright privileges to print our Bibles in the future. If we cannot get permission to use NIV, ESV, NLT, or NKJV, I do not think our target market will purchase our Bibles. (I NEED TO TEST IF VERSION IS AS IMPORTANT AS I BELIEVE IT IS Week 8 test? Maybe features heat map?)

Kanban step 1. Schedule meeting with Mardel.

Kanban step 2. Update pitch and target meeting audience.

Kanban step 3. Write out best case & worst case scenario.

Kanban step 4. Write down on paper what I would like Mardel's help with.

Kanban step 5. Do homework on anyone who will be in the meeting & on Mardel.

Kanban step 6. Appear at meeting early (bask in prayer).

Kanban step 7. Be energetic. Be passionate. Be honest. Make them fall in love with your idea. Make them believe in your vision. Confidently ask what you want their help with.

Kanban step 8. Thank you notes for anyone in meeting.

Kanban step 9. Make sure to follow up with any leads given.

Pass: We walk away from the meeting with: Contact information for a publishing company, another meeting scheduled, plans to meet again after completing assigned task.

Fail: We are turned down because: The idea is not something they believe is worth investing in, something they are pursuing, something they plan to pursue, they prove not to be feasible, or they simply do not want to give any contact information for other companies to us.

Results: We were able to schedule a meeting for the 25th of July. We were also told that we would be put in contact with some of the large publishing companies to discuss possible printing solutions. We validated that Mardel is willing to help us move forward with this venture.

Next Step:
- Celebrate
- Thank you note to Dee Ann Anderson
- Begin putting together presentation material for meeting with Mr. Green
- Contact the publishing companies Mardel gives us

2. **We can bind a copy of Kaleo resources to present to the president of Student Mobilization.**

Why? Because we were told by the regional vice-president we need to have better presentation material for the president.

Kanban step 1. Follow up with Brent Orr.

Kanban step 2. Contact Bonnie Hartwig about digital files.

Kanban step 2. Collect and organize Kaleo binder.

Kanban step 3. Scan each page into computer and organize into file folders.

Kanban step 4. Find pages that will need to be edited and post to Elance.

Edits to look for:
- Anything that is more than 1 page might need to be converted to a .docx and correctly spaced.
- We often took notes on handouts or pulled pages out of the binder to take notes for a specific activity; look for page numbers that are missing and find (might have to have help from someone at Kaleo).

— There might be writing on some of the pages that will need to be removed. The best way might be to upload to Elance and have someone white the writing out.

Kanban step 5. Format pdf document that will print all pages.

Kanban step 6. Print (2 copies).

Kanban step 7. Have Mariah sew into text block.

Kanban step 8. Build cover. CONTACT GREGG FERONTI.

Kanban step 9. Bind.

Kanban step 10. Take pictures!

Next Step: Present to Brent Orr and get his feedback, as well as his help to schedule a meeting with Dave Riner. If he cannot meet with me, ask for his opinion on the prototype via pictures, offer to send him one, ask for changes that could be made, and ask to set up a meeting with Riner. If Brent Orr does not contact me back, go through Brent Reinke or Dagan Flowers to set up a meeting with Riner. Consider asking for feedback from Reinke and Dagan.

3. **We can deliver a 1-page document to 100 people that will ask them exactly what features they would like in their Bible if they could make it themselves and make a heat map of desired features worth investment.**

Why? We will soon need investments to begin production. We have to know the cost of equipment and material before approaching investors. Before moving into the phase where we get quotes on equipment and material, we must know the products we will be producing. We need to know what features to invest in, because if a feature that WE THINK a majority of people will want, but in reality only few do, and it will cost us thousands, tens of thousands, or hundreds of thousands of dollars to produce, we will need to avoid purchasing that equipment. For now.

Kanban step 1. Download a checklist template for Microsoft Word or Excel.

Kanban step 2. Use MakeABible.com binder to transfer itemized categories of features.

Kanban step 3. Create template and save as PDF.

— Look on Elance to have editable PDF created.

Kanban step 4. Print (125 copies).
Kanban step 5. Make list of 125 people to send to.
Kanban step 6. Contact small groups:
— Victory Church (Norman, Edmond, & OKC)
— Summit Church
— Journey Church
Kanban step 7. Distribute survey
Kanban step 8. Collect survey
Kanban step 9. Create heat map (use whiteboard with tally marks)

Icarus Aerial Technologies

This week we needed to find out what quality level of photo would be acceptable to the construction companies that we have previously contacted. Camera quality dictates which camera we use, which in turn dictates which drone to buy. The heavier the camera, in general, the better the picture quality. Another consideration is which type of gymbal to use on the drone. Gymbals are critically important because they can reduce or remove "jello" in your camera footage. Without a gymbal, the footage suffers greatly. Commercial drones are a constantly changing product right now, so gymbals do not exist for all types of cameras. Our choices are between the GoPro Hero 3+ Black Edition and the Sony Nex7. Obviously the Sony has better specs, having a 24 megapixel sensor compared to the 14 megapixel sensor in the GoPro. However, the weight difference is substantial, with the GoPro coming in at 74 grams and the Sony weighing in at 350 grams. This makes a big difference with the drones that we have today.

We set out to see what our potential customers think about the quality of the GoPro stills. To test this, we pulled a high resolution photo off of the internet that was taken with the exact camera that we intend to use for this service. We emailed all of the interested construction companies that were interested in our service a photo of the picture and asked them to provide feedback on the photo. We also printed the photo at Kinkos to be able to show what the picture would look like blown up. The responses we did get back said that the stills looked quality enough for them. It was a little disappointing that the companies we contacted did not all respond to our question to them. However, we feel that the GoPro footage is sufficient for the kind of use that the construction companies need. They have a very utilitarian use for the pictures.

We also wanted to gather more interest from construction companies. Our stated hypothesis was that construction companies would find value in having aerial photos for their personal use. We further tested this again this week, with the test passing if 30% showed interest or called us back. The test failed. We consistently seem to be around the 20% mark instead. It is encouraging that our engagement level increases dramatically when we can get passed the "gatekeeper" at these large companies. Once we are talking to one of the construction managers, the conversation goes well and ends in additional actions (exchange of email and later contact).

Next week we will be operational with the GoPro and the smaller drone, so we can begin photographing the sites.

Park Ave/Project XiP

This past week, the XiP team faced three tests and a big leap forward in technology. While we are still picking up momentum from our shift to serving universities, the team is close to a place where we can put a great looking, functional prototype in front of customers. And trust me, that is a great feeling.

...TESTS...

Here are the three tests we had outlined for last week:
1. If the team orders a proper camera and a Raspberry Pie, we can build a working prototype that can count cars.

2. If we send out the emails, we can schedule two in-person meetings with university parking directors to show them our product.
3. If we pose an up-front cost and a following subscription fee, potential customers would agree to it.

..Results...

1. VALIDATED
2. INVALIDATED
3. INVALIDATED

...Test One...

The most focus has been on this test, and consequentially the best results were reaped here. We have a prototype that works—not only that, but we are a couple days away from finishing weatherproof casing. This will be important when it comes time to sell.

...Test Two...

This was invalidated primarily because of a slow trigger finger. The team sent out the MailChimp several days later than anticipated because we wanted to wait on the technology.

...Test Three...

This was also the victim of waiting for the technology. It's hard for customers to gauge how much they are willing to pay for something until they can clearly see what value they are deriving from the product. Therefore, we kept our conversations with parking directors focused on their problems, not our solution.

...Moving Forward...

The best part about this last week is that the technology is now a reality, thanks to developers that learned Python and dabbled in

Swift over the weekend. Moving forward, it's time to start setting the groundwork for some serious pavement hitting after the 4th of July. It's getting late in the game at the start of week 7, but XiP is starting to really hit its stride.

CLASS 13, WEEK 7—PARTNERS

Partners was the first box on the left side of the business model canvas that we considered, and we therefore started to get a little removed from sales and marketing, my bread and butter. I view the right side of the business model canvas as the "business" side—meaning how you'll test demand for a potential product and then deliver that product to your customers. The left side of the canvas is more about product development, or the technical side of the business. I view that split as quite natural, and it is why many startups have both a business and product cofounder.

Partners can be hard to define, especially for startups, because it feels like the customer development process is one long slog through building partners. But even though you will be working with customers to develop your product, they are not your partner. A true partner would identify you as a partner too!

There are a variety of categories that Steve Blank identifies that a partnership can fall into:

- Strategic alliance

- Competition

- Joint venture

- Buyers

- Suppliers

- Licensees

I consider most of these types of partnerships product-development tools. I approach partnerships, with my marketing mind, from a customer development perspective. In marketing, a partnership can form between two companies that have a similar demographic (customer) but different products—for example, Nike sponsoring a marathon, or a hipster coffee shop hosting a bike repair night.

In developing this kind of partner, a startup needs three skills. The first is identifying a partner who has an overlapping demographic but a different product. This is why it is so critical to have a good sense of who your actual customers are. The second is being able to figure out what it is your partner needs that you can solve. And the third is to pitch them!

In order to pitch a potential partner, you need to be able to explain what is in it for them to work with you. The teams did a practice quick pitch, and the number one improvement needed was to put *first* what is in it for the partner. The first sentence needed to be, "I want to help you do ____."

One of my favorite Steve Blank terms is Earlyvangelists. That's because early-stage startups are in a fight against time to make someone care about what they're doing. Partnerships aren't that important for Earlyvangelists, at least until they start getting some traction. But big companies will often need partners, because it is impossible to be good at doing everything yourself.

CLASS 14, WEEK 7—WRITING FOR THE WEB

At 7 weeks into the program, it was a good moment to look back and see how far 2 months of work can take you. When the teams came in, they were a mix of ideas and business planning, with one team (Levaté) having done a few months of human-centered design. Two months later, there were teams with paid contracts to start pilots with customers, teams with a big list of interested beta testers, teams with high callback percentages from interested university parking directors, teams doing flybys of construction sites, and teams exploring partnerships with large institutions. I was very pleased with the progress created by an obsessive attention to running experiments and hunting for real customer feedback.

In this week's startup skills class, the teams asked for help with how they present their companies in writing. Potential customers often ask for marketing materials. Often the initial point of contact wants information they can pass on to other people inside their company. And folks who get a cold call or email will want to check out a website to learn more about the startup. That's why writing for the web is a critical startup skill. Writing will almost always be how the company introduces itself to potential customers and investors. As the startup progresses, the kind of writing the startup needs will change, owing to the target demographic. A first-time customer learning about the business needs a very different type of writing/marketing program than a long-term repeat customer exploring new offerings.

Here is the one-page worksheet I use to teach writing for the web.

Rules for Writing for the Web

The keys to writing everything: speak fearlessly from the heart, get to the point immediately, keep the message simple and focused, and use the fewest words you can. —Vivek Wadhwa

1. Rule #1: Make your readers care.
2. Add value and educate your readers.
3. Keep your writing short, simple, and substantive.
4. Avoid big words or jargon.
5. Meet your audience where they are (beginner to advanced).
6. Follow your customer's journey, write for all steps of the customer journey.
7. Frequency—Doesn't matter! Be relevant and interesting.
8. Length—like a Miniskirt—long enough to cover the subject, but short enough to keep it interesting.
9. Build editorial calendar, if you want, with themes.
10. Where writing happens:
    a. Social media sites
    b. Emails
    c. Web pages, product pages, apps
    d. Blog
    e. Search results
    f. Intro videos
    g. Tag lines
11. Where writing gets read
    a. Computer
    b. Tablet
    c. Smart phone

Writing checklist—oldies but goodies
- __ Express one idea per paragraph.
- __ Break up blocks with headings and subheadings.
- __ Make headings meaningful (not clever or cute)
- __ Use bullets sparingly (to highlight key details)
- __ Be direct, use the active voice
- __ Use short, declarative sentences (make a statement).

CLASS 14, WEEK 7—WRITING FOR THE WEB

__ Use short, real, everyday words.
__ Write for humans, not machines (how you would actually talk)
__ Be brief with headlines and allow space for resharing the message.
__ Make links count with descriptive keywords.
__ Have a point of view, a personality, CARE about what you're writing about.
__ If you can cut it without changing the meaning of the sentence—cut it.

I find it is much easier to learn to write by actually writing! And the best method for writing for time-pressed startups is time boxing. Time boxing[67] means setting aside a short period (I normally take 15 minutes) to do NOTHING else but write. That means no email, no phone calls, no drinks of water, no walking around the room—*really* just writing. And for first drafts, that means spewing everything that's in your head onto the page. Students are always surprised at how much they can get done in 10 to 15 minutes. In my experience, that's just about enough time to get 500 words out, which is the normal length for a blog post.

After they had written the first draft, and while the content was still in its really raw state, I asked the students to swap with a partner and to analyze their partner's writing, using the checklist from above. Pedagogically, I think it is easier to learn all of these rules through practical application, and it is easier to see the flaws in other peoples' work.

After exchanging commentary, it was time to go back into another timebox (again, 15 minutes was about right) and do a first revision. I asked the students to focus on quality and readability of the ideas. Each and every blog post or writing should take the customer on a journey, carefully laying out stories or arguments or facts. There will be time later (if necessary) to polish grammar, spelling, and punctuation.

The final step is to think about how the writing will be shared on the web. Normally, writing will go on the company's website,

---

67 http://workawesome.com/productivity/timeboxing/

because that's where customers will expect to find information about the product or service. But how will the customer know how to find the content? That's where sharing the writing via social sites, Google (SEO), or email comes into play. The worksheet below is what I used to get the students thinking about the different space and image requirements for each medium.

Channels

What are the different social channels and what are they good for?
1. **Facebook**—Granddaddy. Unlimited users. Create pages for a business or groups. Share all sorts of content, but mostly videos and pictures.
2. **Twitter**—Short messaging service. Have public "private" conversations. Very good as a responsive tool.
3. **LinkedIn**—Platform for your professional self. Useful forums, frequently connected with groups. Highlight your skills for other people to find.
4. **Pinterest**—Very artistic/creative. People can put Pins on Boards. Use to curate what you find interesting, not just to promote your own stuff. People will find and pin good content (all pictures), so take some good pictures.
5. **Instagram**—A photo newsfeed. Similar to Pinterest but less for browsing, more of a newsfeed. Great for sharing photos of your work to your followers. Content gets stale a lot faster.
6. **Google+**—Limited people/traffic, gearing up for SEO impact.

Promote your blog post in different channels.

CLASS 14, WEEK 7—WRITING FOR THE WEB

Facebook (300 characters)

_____
_____
_____
_____
_____

Twitter (140 characters) *(Tip: Leave room for "RT: <user name>")*

_____
_____

Google Search Engine Optimization (Title: 70 characters/Body: 155 characters)

(Title) _____
(Body) _____
_____
_____

Email Subject Line (50 characters)

_____
_____

ACCELERATOR WEEK 7—TEAM BLOG POSTS

As the teams started to focus heavily on preparing their final presentations, their blog posts became pretty light, or they skipped them entirely. From a "building a company" perspective, that isn't so great. But since they were focusing their energies on two significant milestones (lessons-learned presentation and Demo Day), I was okay with the reduced focused on writing during this period.

Levaté

TESTS FOR THE WEEK OF JULY 8TH

- Test 1: Can we build a prototype that is mobile, lifts 300+ lbs a full 12 inches, and can we have a wheelchair user test it?

- Test 2: Can we make progress on funding? This includes submitting an SBIR grant proposal, as well as getting meetings/executing on next steps with 3 potential funding contacts we have.

- Test 3: Can we make a short video comprised of prototyping footage and customer interviews that we could use for a kickstarter campaign?

Sowers Publishing

Updates from India!

Hi Cooper and Eric! I just wanted to check in and give you some updates on things I've been learning for our company during my time in India.

ACCELERATOR WEEK 7—TEAM BLOG POSTS

1. The organization I'm here with is currently working on translating and copyrighting an entire version of the Bible. They have already completed the New Testament and have printed versions of them but they are really poor quality. What is exciting about this is that they are translating a version of the Bible that is in the language of the 1.2 billion people who currently reside in India. The need for this version is small right now but it is multiplying every single year. Because this version is new and the copyrighting hasn't been completed yet, we have the opportunity to work with this ministry and present our idea and hopefully be a part of the printing and designing of the first Bibles designed specifically for Hindi-speaking Yeshu bhaktas (Jesus followers)!
2. The missionaries who live here full time are essentially "under cover." There are many stereotypes associated with being a Christian in India, which is why the missionaries who live here have contextualized their lives and worship to the point that they no longer identify themselves as Christians, but as Hindus who follow Yeshu (Jesus) as their only God. With that being said, they cannot take their Bible anywhere with them in public for fear that they will be labeled as a "Christian." Knowing this, we can move forward with Bibles designed specifically for these people that look like regular books. With Bibles designed like this, they can take them in their backpacks and to coffee shops like Starbucks and not have to worry about people knowing what they are reading. Because of a violent history with Pakistan that includes several bombings, there is security that includes a bag search, a metal detector, and sometimes even a pat down/wand to enter almost every business in India. This includes every mall, restaurant, Starbucks, coffee shop, etc. This means that these people can't even carry their Bible around with them in their backpack or purse because they are checked every single time they go into a building. A more inconspicuous design would eliminate this problem for them.

3. The "holy color" in India is orange, so all religious books are printed with orange covers. This is good information for us to have if we decide to print any kind of Bibles in the Hindi translation because it is more meaningful to Indians culturally.
4. Indians learn through stories. Their religious views have been passed down to them via stories from their grandparents and parents, and very few of them have actually ever opened one of their holy books to read for themselves. With that being said, there would have to be a cultural change that takes place for Yeshu bhaktas to begin learning about the Bible by reading it themselves instead of hearing it in story form from their family members.
5. Any foreign owned company that does business in India must be 51% owned by an Indian company, which is why a lot of major companies still have not come here even though they will soon have the largest population in the world. It is also really difficult to do business in India because the government is extremely corrupt and the process is quite lengthy to establish your business unless you want to bribe a lot of people on the way.
6. I'm not sure I can do business in India because their culture as a whole has no sense of urgency and the businesses are run really inefficiently…I cringe just thinking about how many empty stores I've walked into in the malls with 15+ employees just standing around. But I've also learned that the cost of labor is ridiculously cheap.
7. Indian food is really spicy.

CLASS 15, WEEK 8—RESOURCES, ACTIVITIES, AND COSTS

The seventh Lean Launchpad class is the last one of the curriculum. It looks at the key activities and resources and how much it will cost to make the product the business sells. Being on the left side of the business model canvas means I consider it part of the "product" side of the startup equation. One basic assumption I had going into the Accelerator was that if a team could prove there was a market for their product, a demand for it, then they would be able to build it. Building would require people and resources, but those aren't in short supply if you have the money to pay for them. And if a startup can prove that customers are willing to pay for the product, they can normally find the money to pay for the resources to build the product.

All of the work the teams did to validate their market answers the first startup question: does anyone want to buy or use what I'm making? That goes by the handy name of product-market fit.

The second question is, can I make money selling the product or service that people want? That gets into all the questions of customers and channels, culminating in the revenue box on the business model canvas.

The third question is whether the business makes enough money to be worth the trouble of operating it. Costs are the critical piece of the puzzle here. If people are willing to pay for a product, are they willing to pay enough to generate the surplus needed to pay for the folks and equipment who make the product and have enough left over to return the founders' and investors' capital contributions?

It took 7 weeks to get through the business model canvas using the Lean Launchpad curriculum, and I believe by the end, the teams had an understanding of what it takes to put a business together. In many ways, running the Summer Accelerator was its own startup experiment, testing whether running teams through weekly cycles of Lean Startup–style experiments[68] and a startup-skills curriculum would be effective. And by effective, I mean, could they find people willing to pay for (or at least use) their product?

Coming into the Accelerator, none of the teams had asked for any firm commitments from their customers. That's a big piece to be missing! By the end of the summer, we had quite a bit of success in that area. Driven Analytics had a paid pilot with two dealerships. Levaté had 150 people signed up to be beta testers. Project Xip (né Park Ave) had a $10,000 grant from the University of Oklahoma's parking director to run a proof of concept. Icarus had done test flights with construction agencies and had delivered photographs.

In my estimation, that's a fair amount of progress to have made in 2 months. And that's just from the business side. From the academic side, the students have been exposed to, and used, a variety of methodologies that are very much in vogue in the business world, particularly Agile and Lean. They also have experience in using the business model canvas and a Kanban board. They learned how to make weekly commitments and stick to them to keep momentum always moving forward. They learned how to deal with outside investment, form a company, negotiate among founders, track cash inflows and outflows, build and test a sales channel, and how to close a customer. And most importantly, in my estimation, they learned how to truly validate whether an idea holds water and to make the tough decisions about whether to pursue ideas or change to new ones (pivot or persevere).

After week 8, two main activities remained—Lessons Learned and Demo Day presentations. The teams needed to pull together all their learnings, all their experiments, and all their progress for

---

68 For more on this topic, see the chapter, **MVP examples from the real world.**

CLASS 15, WEEK 8—RESOURCES, ACTIVITIES, AND COSTS

presentations. Quite a few folks came to Demo Day, so the teams had a strong audience full of critical thinkers in the entrepreneurship space.

With respect to presenting their ideas in a formal manner, by this point in the summer the teams have had to officially pitch their business at least once a week at the team dinner as well as in one class we held midway through on pitching. They've also had a storyboarding class that helped them think through the flow of a pitch. And last but not least, they had to think of how they would pitch their business almost every single day when talking to potential customers, clients, partners, and investors.

FROM LAUNCH PAD TO DEMO DAY

In between class 15 on Resources and Costs and Demo Day, the students had three classes and two dinners remaining.

For the first of the two dinners we went to Jeff Moore's house (he's the director of CCEW) for a BBQ. I invited Danny Maloney, CEO and cofounder of Tailwind, as well as investors who work with i2e to talk about how the deal that funded Tailwind came together. I found it pretty compelling to hear how both sides of the deal positioned themselves and what they were trying to get out of it. In the end it was pretty simple—the company needed cash to grow quickly, and the investors wanted a return on their capital. Underneath that, though, there was some interesting conversation about the traction a company needs to find before taking on investment and what kind of traction the investor wants to see to reduce the risk before making the investment.

Risk was definitely the word of the evening, and it jived very neatly with what the Accelerator and Lean Startup are all about. Entrepreneurship is inherently about taking risks. But that doesn't mean the entrepreneur should be reckless, and I think the best entrepreneurs aren't even big risk-takers at all (see *Little Bets*[69] again). Verifying demand and following the money will allow the entrepreneur to build things people want to buy. At some point the company will have to grow and scale and face new challenges, but that comes after product-market fit.

In the next class (Class 16, Week 8), Pat Jones from Petra Industries came in to introduce the students to entrepreneurial accounting. We started with a fairly simple read to get some of the accounting terms

---

[69] http://www.amazon.com/dp/B0043RSJTU/?tag=ericmorrow-20

down—*Accounting Made Simple*[70]. While the shortest book I can find, it didn't bring this relatively staid subject to life enough. Pat's stories from his adventures at Hobby Lobby and Petra provided a much needed boost.

Class 17 was group pitch feedback. The teams came in with their Demo Day–ready pitches to get feedback from the group.

Our last team dinner, between Class 17 and 18, was the rehearsal dinner. Everything was set up to resemble what Demo Day will look like at the CCEW offices, where the pitches would be held. The teams used the projector that they'll use on Demo Day. And Reese Travis, CEO of Orange Leaf Yogurt, came in to give the teams feedback. All in all, I felt the teams were fairly close to ready for Demo Day and that with one more week of revisions, they'd give a good showing.

At our last startup skills class, Class 18, we looked at financial modeling. Doug Woodward, formerly of Oracle and Microsoft, taught the teams just enough to be dangerous as CEOs of their organizations. Here's the spreadsheet he used as an example:

Small Biz Forum – Seminar Business Model 07 17 2014[71]

Financial modeling is something I don't know much about, so I particularly enjoyed this class! As a sales and marketing guy, I normally think about how to acquire customers and sell them a product. The financial model shows how the business will make money as a whole.

To me, financial modeling seems the natural next step *after* the business model canvas. If we go all the way back to day 1 of the Accelerator, the students drew out their business model and then transferred that to the business model canvas. The canvas is perfect for tracking assumptions about the business. And as we went through the Accelerator, we validated those assumptions or invalidated them and made new ones. Eventually the business model should be fairly well validated and can be shown to investors and the internal team on spreadsheet in the form of a financial model.

---

70 http://www.amazon.com/dp/0981454224/?tag=ericmorrow-20
71 http://ericmorrow.com/wp-content/uploads/Small-Biz-Forum-Seminar-Business-Model-07-17-2014.xlsx

In the final class, the teams gave their lessons-learned presentations. The purpose of the presentations is for the teams to reflect on what they learned in the previous 9 weeks and for me to learn what worked when I taught it (because the students found it useful) and what didn't. The director of the Entrepreneurship program, Jim Wheeler, sat in on the presentations.

After that, the last stop on this train was Demo Day! The teams would present their pitches and wrap up with conversations with the audience and lunch. It has been a wild summer!

LESSONS LEARNED

Steve Blank uses the last official class session to have the teams present their lessons learned. Here are his exact instructions on how to prepare a lessons-learned video, copied directly from the Lean Launchpad. I thought the instructions were so good that I could not further improve on them. And from the quality of the responses, it seems that was a good instinct to have.

Note: The following is taken from Blank's *Lean Launchpad Educator's Guide,* which you can find in its entirety here.[72]

Loads of examples and info for lessons learned

http://www.youtube.com/watch?v=ZyGr-eoONqo
http://www.youtube.com/watch?v=7bJ8rd1dxy8
http://www.youtube.com/watch?v=S7H0LZWVt0I

1, RedOx team from Yale:
http://www.slideshare.net/sblank/redox-final-nsf-presentation
2. NeonLabs from Carnegie Mellon University:
http://www.slideshare.net/sblank/lighttip-nsf-final-presentation
3. Phioptics from the University of Illinois:
http://www.slideshare.net/sblank/phioptics-nsf-final-presentation
4. OmegaChem Iowa State University:
http://www.slideshare.net/sblank/omegachem-nsf-final-presentation
5. City Climber team from City University of New York:
http://www.slideshare.net/sblank/city-climber-story-video-nsf
6. Soliculture team from UC Santa Cruz:

---

72 http://www.nciia.org/sites/default/files/u7/Educators%20Guide%20Jan%202014.pdf

http://www.slideshare.net/sblank/soliculture-story-video-nsf

Story Video Details (2 minutes)

If I can replace your team name and get the same story, that is BAD! Be unique! Be very specific! (*note: my addition, the rest is from Steve Blank's curriculum*)

Think of the story video as the heart of the team presentation as told through video.

Suggested Story Video outline:

- What are your names and what is your team's name? Introduce yourselves. Pan the camera around your office so we can see where you work.

- How many customers did you talk to?

- Did you find this easy? Hard at first?

- When you started the class, what was the most important thing you thought you would have to do to successfully launch a scalable startup?

- How do you feel about that now?

- Thinking back across the class, who was the most interesting customer you met and where did you meet them?

- What happened?

- Why, specifically, was this your most interesting customer conversation?

- And how, specifically, did your business model change as a result?

- Now that the class is over, what was the most surprising thing you learned in the class?

Lessons Learned PowerPoint Presentation (8 minutes)

The "lessons learned" slide deck is a very short list of definitions and simple declaratives that are intended to increase the quality of the presentations. Here it is, in full:

- Story.
- Be specific.
- Show me, don't tell me.
- Arcs.
- Beginning, middle, end.
- Character, setting, plot.
- Editing.
- Notes.
- Look before…
- Practice!
- Be specific.
- Use (or enhance) the diagrams you developed in weekly presentations to illustrate these points.

Common Student Errors: Presentation and Video

Students often make very bland story videos:

- They don't naturally hone in and choose very specific details of their technology, their customers, and their learning process. This is essential—the more specific, the better. (*Note: I overemphasized this part. I wanted very specific details about what the students did over the summer.*)

- It is only through the specificity of a storyteller that an audience can extrapolate to generality, which is what teams would want an investor to do. Students often spend time thanking instructors, speaking excitedly about the Lean Launchpad program, or making cheeky references or inside jokes. This is a huge mistake, and can make their presentation feel like a junior high school Science Fair project. Students should spend absolutely zero time on any of these topics, and all meta references to how important teamwork is should be aggressively cut. This is very hard for many students to internalize.

- None of that has any place in a 2-minute video about a real company that is actually trying to raise real money from real investors. Investors will ascertain team dynamics for themselves when they meet a company and get to know the people involved. Students think they need to tell a whitewashed success story: This is another big mistake, and will damage their attempts at getting subsequent financing.

- Students must strive to tell the authentic, honest story of their successes and mistakes, pitfalls, discoveries, and pivots.

- Most importantly, students must talk in the most specific terms possible about the customers they actually met, what they actually said, and how that changed their Business Model Canvases.

Lessons-Learned Presentations

The links below will take you to the videos the students prepared for their lessons-learned presentations, the actual lessons-learned presentations themselves, and the Demo Day presentations. For a collection of these videos in one easy-to-watch place on the web, please visit my blog.[73]

1. **Driven Analytics** view presentations (video)

---

[73] http://ericmorrow.com/2014/08/07/videos-ou-accelerator-lessons-learned-demo-day/

LESSONS LEARNED

2. **Levaté** view presentations (video)
3. **Icarus Aerial Technologies** view presentations (video)
4. **XiP Technologies** view presentations (video)
5. **Sower Publishing Group** view presentations (video)

My thoughts on what the students said they learned

The first thing I thought when I saw the final presentations was, "wow!" I was blown away by the quality of the videos, the presentations, and what the students said they learned. There was a heavy emphasis placed on *really* listening to customers, selling and scaling/scrambling/building, and Elaine Hamm from i2e identifying good challenges to the businesses.

Also:

- Learn who your customer is by trying to sell them (getting out of the building).

- Spend time with your customer learning about them.

- Seize *unexpected* opportunities that arise!

- Research and talking alone doesn't find customers.

- Cash validation is powerful validation.

- Look for shark bite interest (vs. mosquito bite).

- Power of the prototype—show people your device actually working (pictures/videos/real life).

- Power of cold calling—hunt down your customers.

- Testing the market by selling and looking for commitments is more effective than relying on people's excitement.

- You need to verify and validate that the personal pain you feel is also felt by others.

- Fear is limiting and prevents you from learning.

My lessons learned from running my first Accelerator

The teams invited me to one last get-together after the Demo Day on Thursday morning. Besides giving me two awesome farewell gifts (a cowboy hat and a Thunder t-shirt), they also gave me a lot of feedback on the program. Here is what I want to work on for the Accelerator program.

Making classes more collaborative—A lot of class time was spent working within a team on preparing experiments and doing exercises. Next time I'll shuffle up the teams during class a bit more to encourage the exchange of ideas.

How to build a sales and marketing funnel—We spent a fair bit of time on this during class, but there was a demand for more information. I think these class sessions could have had expanded hours.

Put learning to talk to customers earlier—The teams wanted more training with talking to customers earlier on. I think this is a bit of a chicken-and- egg thing. The students only knew they needed to get better after spending a few weeks talking to people and not being happy with the results.

Preload legal, so hit the ground running on Day 1—The legal matters did dominate the first few weeks of the Accelerator. However, all the documents are now available, and this problem should be resolved for the next iteration.

Get word out sooner—Similar to the legal issues, now that we have done the Accelerator once, advertising has already begun for next summer's iteration.

Going to an art museum or other creative place—The summer was intensely focused on running experiments. I think there could be other opportunities, outside of the team dinners, where the students could have mingled with each other in different environments. I would like to introduce more activities into future iterations of the Accelerator. Also, possibly take a team trip.

Getting people's feedback on the design of the experiment, or as a whole—This was a big piece of feedback and pointed to my overinvolvement in the critique of an experiment. Next time I need to do a better job stepping back and allowing the teams to self-critique.

Purpose of the blog—I was not clear with the purpose of the team's blog. The teams understood it to be purely for documentation of each week's experiments. Instead, it was meant to track the startup's progress over the life of the Accelerator. Now that I have some example blogs to share with the next Accelerator class, I think this issue will be easy to resolve. The students said to say to future students:

- Document your thoughts on the blog.

- Use it as a time line about what you're working on.

- Lessons-learned log book.

- Describe what you're trying to solve and what you're trying to learn.

- Include your experiments.

Standard way of teaching guest classes—Each guest class ended up being a bit different, and the more effective ones were where the guest teacher worked with me on the curriculum. Good classes are exercise-based, but this is not how everyone prepares for a class. The students also asked for office hours with the outside teachers to complement the classroom component. That way each team could get more personalized advice from the people coming in to teach.

Big format canvases—One comment from week one was that we filled out the canvas on 8.5 x 11 paper, and that was too small to be helpful. So one of the team members went to the print shop and printed out a medium-size version and a large version. The test was to see which paper the students took to actually work on, and the jumbo-size one won hands down! It was much better for sticky notes, which meant rather than literally rewriting the canvas each week, just the sticky notes could be updated.

Office hours—Office hours were barely used over the summer. I think having the Accelerator in this format , where we were already seeing each other three times a week, that extra office hours were not needed.

DEMO DAY

The culmination of the Summer Accelerator was Demo Day. I sent an eventbrite[74] to everyone who was involved with the teams over the summer, inviting them to come watch the teams pitch.

Our Demo Day followed a simple structure: I made a brief welcome and introduction of the program. Then the five teams each made a presentation. Each team had 7 minutes to pitch their business, followed by three questions from the audience, with 45 seconds allotted per response. After the pitches, there was an open mingle session.

The purpose of the Demo Day was to have a concrete goal and end date the startups are working towards. The Accelerator provided a set structure for the startup to operate in, until the business got actual customers and developed its own internal rhythms by catering to them. The Demo Day marked the end of the Accelerator and was the moment when the startup should have had enough traction to go out into the world and continue making progress on its own steam.

Conclusion

Much like a startup, I came into the Accelerator program with many assumptions. One critical one was that I could engage the teams enough that they would follow my program for 10 weeks. The second one was that the methodology I wanted to teach would be successful at getting customer traction. And the third was that the startups would learn and grow fast enough over the 10 weeks that there would be a clear

---

74 http://ouaccelerator.eventbrite.com

path forward coming out of the Accelerator. I feel comfortable saying that all three assumptions were validated. Check out the Demo Day videos to see the results for yourself! All of the videos are available for easy viewing on my blog: http://ericmorrow.com/2014/08/07/videos-ou-accelerator-lessons-learned-demo-day/[75]

Engagement

I didn't offer any grades for the Accelerator. The only true grade was whether the team could create (or be on the road to creating) a viable business. The teams came to class every week and discussed their experiments and what they were learning. The students actively participated in class and shared their experiences. Every visitor to the program remarked on how committed the students seemed to be. Ultimately, I think the pace and content of the classes were relevant for the students, and they stuck with the program for the duration.

Methodology

When the five teams came in, they were in a variety of stages, but generally "pre-reality." That meant they had brainstormed ideas, maybe talked to some interested customers, but hadn't ever tried to sell their product or get people to use their service. And that's the rub—people will often say all sorts of nice things until you ask them to open their wallet, at which point the answer is often, "sorry, not interested."

So the challenge of the Accelerator was to get all of the teams' ideas tested and validated as rapidly as possible. And I believe my methodology of combining week-long sprints with experiential prototypes proved effective. Teams were able to get good feedback on their ideas—often negative, of course—and were able to pivot quickly, looking for an idea that got a good customer response. And they were trained to be able to recognize a valid customer response

---

75 http://ericmorrow.com/2014/08/07/videos-ou-accelerator-lessons-learned-demo-day/

(the commitment of money or time to the project) versus an invalid customer response (saying they liked the idea).

Clear path forward

With pilots in place for every team, it is clear what they have to do next. The challenge will be to extract useful information from the pilots and continue to build products and services that appeal to the customers. Some of the businesses are even getting close to being investment ready, with i2e (a local investment group) asking to speak to several of the teams. My personal belief is that most could continue to bootstrap to profitability, meaning they could run their companies on the basis of profits earned from paying customers without taking outside investment.

What an experience!

In the end, this was a tremendously rewarding experience for me, both personally and professionally. It was fantastic working with the teams week in and week out. It was great seeing them apply Lean and Agile principles to find and grow customer interest. It was wonderful seeing my ideas and assumptions in action and discovering that they were effective. And even more interesting was seeing some of my own early teaching ideas get invalidated because they were cumbersome and ineffective. Thanks to OU for the opportunity. And thank you for coming along this journey with me!

LIFE AFTER THE ACCELERATOR

One big task for the teams once the Accelerator came to an end was how to maintain their forward progress without the Accelerator's structure. They decided to get together once every 2 weeks to update each other on their progress, following the same experiment-presentation format we followed all summer. Here are the videos from their first meeting.
https://www.youtube.com/watch?v=St2BhIbOLUs&index=1&list=UUkF15cryQX70LdwArlENECA[76]

They are planning to get together all semester long. I said if they make it to ten meetings, I'll fly back to Oklahoma and take them out to celebrate!

---

[76] https://www.youtube.com/watch?v=St2BhIbOLUs&index=1&list=UUkF15cryQX70LdwArlENECA

ACKNOWLEDGMENTS

There are so many people who helped in making the Accelerator possible over the summer of 2014 and in making this book possible, to whom I am extremely grateful:

- Students in the program who worked hard to build companies
- Mentors who guided them
- Dinner guests who shared their stories and provided feedback on the pitches
- Guest teachers who shared their expertise
- Jim Wheeler, for making it all happen, and the rest of the folks at OU
- Marji Gold and Dillon Carroll, for slogging through early editions of the book to provide crucial feedback
- Adi Segal and Dave Terry, for being powerhouse editors

APPENDIX

Startup pitch decks resources

I recently did some research on the current state of affairs in startup pitch decks. Here are some examples I found that are good starting points/ideas for discussion.

Startup pitch decks for inspiration

- Facebook—http://digiday.com/platforms/how-eduardo-saverin-sold-facebook-ads-in-2004/
- Foursquare—http://www.businessinsider.com/this-is-the-first-pitch-deck-foursquare-ever-showed-investors-2011-12?op=1
- Mint—http://www.slideshare.net/hnshah/mintcom-prelaunch-pitch-deck
- Airbnb—http://www.businessinsider.com/airbnb-a-13-billion-dollar-startups-first-ever-pitch-deck-2011-9#-1
- Everest—http://evr.st/investors
- Piffle—http://pitch.csspiffle.com/#intro

Some general links I found helpful as well:

- http://jonbischke.com/2009/11/13/a-dozen-of-the-best-start-up-pitches-on-the-web/

- http://www.quora.com/Whats-the-best-VC-pitch-deck-or-video-that-I-can-see-online

And the best advice I saw on making a pitch deck:

- http://blog.guykawasaki.com/2005/12/the_102030_rule.html

www.ingramcontent.com/pod-product-compliance
Lightning Source LLC
Chambersburg PA
CBHW051805170526
45167CB00005B/1883